I0809880

LifeLight

"In Him was life, and that life was the light of men." John 1:4

Hebrews

LEADERS GUIDE

CONCORDIA PUBLISHING HOUSE • SAINT LOUIS

3558 S. Jefferson Ave., St. Louis, MO 63118-3968
1-800-325-3040 • cph.org

Earl H. Gaulke, editor

Revised from material prepared by Jonathan Grothe and Arnold Kuntz

Scripture quotations marked KJV are from the King James or Authorized Version of the Bible.

This publication may be available in Braille, in large print, or on cassette tape for the visually impaired. Please allow 8 to 12 weeks for delivery. Write to Lutheran Braille Workers, P.O. Box 5000, Yucaipa, CA 92399; call toll-free 1-800-925-6092; or visit the website: www.LBWinc.org.

Manufactured in the U.S.A.

Cover illustration, Rafael Lopez

7 8 9 10 11 12 29 28 27 26 25 24

Contents

Introduction

Welcome to LifeLight

A special pleasure is in store for you. You will be instrumental in leading your brothers and sisters in Christ closer to Him who is our life and light (John 1:4). You will have the pleasure of seeing fellow Christians discover new insights and rediscover old ones as they open the Scriptures and dig deep into them, perhaps deeper than they have ever dug before. More than that, you will have the pleasure of sharing in this wonderful study.

LifeLight—An In-depth Study

LifeLight is a series of in-depth Bible studies. The goal of LifeLight is that through a regular program of in-depth personal and group study of Scripture, more and more Christian adults may grow in their personal faith in Jesus Christ, enjoy fellowship with the members of His body, and reach out in love to others in witness and service.

In-depth means that this Bible study includes the following four components: individual daily home study; discussion in a small group; a lecture presentation on the Scripture portion under study; and an enhancement of the week's material (through reading the enrichment magazine).

LifeLight Participants

LifeLight participants are adults who desire a deeper study of the Scriptures than is available in the typical Sunday morning adult Bible class. (Mid-to-older teens might also be LifeLight participants.) While LifeLight does not assume an existing knowledge of the Bible or special experience or skills in Bible study, it does assume a level of commitment that will bring participants to each of the nine weekly assemblies having read the assigned readings and attempted to answer the study questions. Daily reading and study will require from 15 to 30 minutes for the five days preceding the LifeLight assembly. The day following the assembly will be spent reviewing the previous week's study by going over the completed study leaflet and the enrichment magazine.

LifeLight Leadership

While the in-depth process used by LifeLight begins with individual study and cannot achieve its aims without this individual effort, it cannot be completed by individual study alone. Therefore, trained leaders are necessary. You fill one or perhaps more of the important roles described below.

The Director

This person oversees the LifeLight program in a local center (which may be a congregation or a center operated by several neighboring congregations). The director

- serves as the parish LifeLight overall coordinator and leader;
- coordinates the scheduling of the LifeLight program;
- orders materials;
- convenes LifeLight leadership team meetings;
- develops publicity materials;
- recruits participants;
- maintains records and budgeting;
- assigns, with the leadership team, participants to small discussion groups;
- makes arrangements for facilities;
- communicates outreach opportunities to small-group leaders and to congregational boards;
- follows up on participants who leave the program.

The Assistant Director *(optional)*

This person may assist the director. Duties listed for the director may be assigned to the assistant director as mutually agreeable.

The Lecture Leader

This person prepares and delivers the lecture at the weekly assembly. **(Lesson material for the lecture leader begins on p. 7.)** The lecture leader

- prepares and presents the Bible study lecture to the large group;
- prepares worship activities (devotional thought, hymn, prayer), using resources in the study leaflet and leaders guide and possibly other outside sources;
- helps the small-group discussion leaders to grow in understanding the content of the lessons;
- encourages prayer at weekly leadership-team and discussion-leaders meetings.

The Small-Group Coordinator *(optional; the director may fill this role)*

This person supervises and coordinates the work of the small-group discussion leaders. The small-group coordinator

- recruits with the leadership team the small-group discussion leaders;
- trains or arranges for training of the discussion leaders;
- assists the director and discussion leaders in follow-up and outreach;
- encourages the discussion leaders to contact absent group members;
- participates in the weekly leadership-team and discussion-leaders equipping meetings;
- provides ongoing training and support as needed.

The Small-Group Discussion Leaders

These people guide and facilitate discussion of LifeLight participants in the small groups. **(Lesson material for the small-group leaders begins on p. 00.)** There should be one discussion leader for every group of no more than 12 participants. The small-group discussion leaders are, perhaps, those individuals who are most important to the success of the program. They should, therefore, be chosen with special care and be equipped with skills needed to guide discussion and to foster a caring fellowship within the group. These discussion leaders

- prepare each week for the small-group discussion by using the study leaflet and small-group leaders guide section for that session **(see p. 63)**;
- read the enrichment magazine as a study supplement;
- guide and facilitate discussion in their small group;
- encourage and assist the discussion group in prayer;
- foster fellowship and mutual care within the discussion group;
- attend weekly discussion-leaders training meetings.

Leadership Training

LifeLight leaders will meet weekly to review the previous week's work and plan the coming week. At this session, leaders can address concerns and prepare for the coming session. LifeLight is a 1½-hour program with no possibility for it to be taught in the one hour typically available on Sunday mornings. Some congregations, however, may want to use the Sunday morning Bible study hour for LifeLight preparation and leadership training. In such a meeting, the lecture leader and/or small-group coordinator may lead the discussion leaders through the coming week's lesson, reserving 5 or 10 minutes for problem solving or other group concerns.

While it requires intense effort, LifeLight has proven to bring great benefit to LifeLight participants. The effort put into this program, both by leaders and by participants, will be rewarding and profitable.

The LifeLight Weekly Schedule

Here is how LifeLight will work week by week:

1. Before session 1, each participant will receive the study leaflet for session 1 and the enrichment magazine for the course. The study leaflet contains worship resources (for use both in individual daily study and at the opening of the following week's assembly) and readings and study questions for five days. Challenge questions will lead those participants who have the time and desire a greater challenge into even deeper levels of study.
2. After the five days of individual study at home, participants will gather for a weekly assembly of all LifeLight participants. The assembly will begin with a brief period of worship (5 minutes). Participants will then join their assigned small discussion groups (of 12 or fewer, who will remain the same throughout the course), where they will go over the week's

study questions together (55 minutes). Assembling together once again, participants will listen to a lecture presentation on the readings they have studied in the previous week and discussed in their small groups (20 minutes). After the lecture presentation, the director or another leader will distribute the study leaflet for the following week. Closing announcements and other necessary business may take another five minutes before dismissal.

In some places some small groups will not join the weekly assembly because of scheduling or other reasons. Such groups may meet at another time and place (perhaps in the home of one of the small group's members). They will follow the same schedule. The discussion leader will obtain the leaflets from the director. The congregation may record the lecture given by the lecture leader at the weekly assembly and duplicate it for use by other groups meeting later in the week.

3. On the day following the assembly, participants will review the preceding week's work by rereading the study leaflet they completed (and that they perhaps supplemented or corrected during the discussion in their small group) and by reading appropriate articles in the enrichment magazine.

Then the LifeLight weekly study process will begin all over again!

Recommended Study Resources for Hebrews

The Lutheran Study Bible, English Standard Version. St. Louis: Concordia Publishing House, 2009. This Bible contains over 26,500 uniquely Lutheran study notes; over 80,000 cross-references; 120 full or half-page maps, charts, and diagrams; 220-plus articles and introductions to Biblical books and topics; and 31,000 concordance entries.

Kleinig, John. *Concordia Commentary: Hebrews.* St. Louis: Concordia Publishing House, 2017. This commentary by emeritus professor of exegetical theology in Australian Lutheran College (formerly Luther Seminary) in Adelaide, Australia proposes an interpretation that uses a new kind of liturgical rhetoric, and a new consideration of the context and purpose of the homily known as the book of Hebrews.

Bruce, F. F. *The Epistle to the Hebrews* (NICNT). Grand Rapids, MI: Eerdmans, 1964; revised and enlarged, 1990. A helpful resource, carefully expounds the many analogies drawing heavily on the Old Testament and their fulfillment in Christ (typology).

Concordia Self-Study Bible, New International Version. St. Louis: Concordia Publishing House, 1986. Interpretive notes on each page form a running commentary on the text. The book includes cross-references, a 35,000-word concordance, full-color maps, charts, and timelines.

Guthrie, Donald. *The Letter to the Hebrews: An Introduction and Commentary* (TNTC). Grand Rapids: Eerdmans, 1983. Comments on the Christological emphases of Hebrews.

Lauersdorf, Richard E. *Hebrews* (People's Bible Commentary Series). Milwaukee: Northwestern Publishing House, 1986. Reprinted by Concordia Publishing House, 1992. A "readable" commentary that avoids technical jargon.

Lenski, R. C. H. *The Interpretation of the Epistle to the Hebrews and of the Epistle of James.* Minneapolis: Augsburg Publishing House, 1966. A lucid exposition with emphasis on the Christological themes of the writer of Hebrews. Careful attention to typology.

Roehrs, Walter R., and Martin H. Franzmann. *Concordia Self-Study Commentary.* St. Louis: Concordia Publishing House, 1979. An invaluable one-volume commentary on the Bible.

Westcott, B. F. *A Commentary on the Epistle to the Hebrews.* Grand Rapids: Eerdmans, 1950 reprint. Although somewhat old, still a helpful resource with special reference to the Greek and the early church fathers.

Every Voice a Song: Pipe Organ Accompaniment for 180 Hymns and Liturgy. St. Louis: Concordia Publishing House (order no. 99-1565). Use this music CD for worship hymn accompaniment.

Listen to the Son

Hebrews 1–2

Preparing for the Session

Central Focus

We are like pilgrims who need a word of encouragement; Hebrews encourages us to listen to the Word of God revealed in the Son of God, Jesus.

Objectives

That participants, led by the Holy Spirit, will

1. recognize that Jesus is the decisive revelation of God to us;
2. be aware of angels as the servants of God for our sake;
3. be confident that Jesus has overcome the power of the devil, sin, and death by His perfect completion of all that is required for our salvation;
4. honor and worship Jesus as the Son of God.

Note for the small-group leaders: Lesson notes and other materials you will need begin on page 00.

For the Lecture Leader

Bible Background

Ordinarily, authors of New Testament epistles identify themselves. Not so in the case of Hebrews; it is anonymous. (The superscriptions and titles in printed Bibles are the work of collectors and editors, not part of the inspired record.) Nor do we know for certain the persons to whom it was first addressed. "To the Hebrews," the title added in the second century A.D., could mean "Jews," "Jewish Christians," or "Christians of a particular Jewish background." It is a good hypothesis that a Hellenistic Jewish Christian teacher (Luther suggested Apollos) sent this message to a separatist group of Jewish Christians in Rome shortly before A.D. 70.

While it is desirable to have a workable hypothesis, to be certain about the author and original historical situation is not essential. But it is good to recognize the form and value of the document. Hebrews is a word of exhortation, a homily, a first-century sermon sent by mail. It has strengthened the faith and encouraged the perseverance of many generations of believers.

Throughout Hebrews, exhortation (encouragement) and doctrine (teaching, assertions) alternate. While many students of Hebrews have been fascinated with its doctrinal assertions about Jesus Christ, we are convinced that the exhortations are the author's main points and the doctrinal sections present the basis of the encouragement—the reasons why the readers should do what the author says. Those doctrinal sections make assertions about Jesus as the fulfillment of what was revealed in the Old Testament period.

Thus the doctrinal sections are constantly accompanied by references to Old Testament passages and discussions of how the Old Testament itself points forward to Jesus. This use of the Old Testament shows how important Holy Scripture was to the first readers and how important the correct (Christ-centered) interpretation of the Old Testament is. The portions of the Old Testament most often referred to are the Pentateuch and the Psalms. Of special interest for review are Genesis 14, Exodus 25–26, Leviticus 16, Deuteronomy 4, and Psalms 2, 8, 95, and 110. Jeremiah 31 is also an important passage.

Session Plan

Worship

Begin the session with the hymn printed in the study leaflet. Accompaniments are available in denominational hymnals, such as *Lutheran Worship* (refer to hymnal index). Note: Concordia Publishing House has available *Every Voice a Song,* a 9-CD set of organ accompaniments for 180 hymns and liturgy. All the initial worship hymns in the LifeLight courses are included in this resource. It's especially helpful for mission congregations and small parishes. See the list of study resources on page 7.

Devotion

Read aloud or (preferably) put into your own words the following brief devotional message.

As we know by our own experience, listening is sometimes difficult and is often hard work. I mean, *really* listening. Failure to communicate damages and sometimes destroys relationships. Failure to communicate sometimes comes when people don't talk to one another; more often, it comes when people don't listen to one another.

In this first section of the Letter to the Hebrews, we are encouraged to listen—to listen to Jesus, the Son of God. If listening is important for preserving our everyday relationships with other people, it is even more important for preserving our most important relationship of all—our relationship with the Lord. The consequences of failing to listen to the Lord are far more terrible than those of failing to listen to another person. For only with the Lord do we find grace, grace that gives us life, life that never ends but takes us from this world to the next.

So listen! Listen to the Son!

Pray together the prayer printed in the study leaflet.

Lecture Presentation

1 Introduction—Pilgrims: Receive This Word of Encouragement

A. Christians Are Pilgrims

"I'm but a stranger here, heaven is my home"—so we sing in a popular hymn. When we sing the words of that hymn, we are saying that we don't belong to this earth, that we are just passing through on our way to another destination—heaven—where our permanent home is located. We Christians know we are pilgrims on this earth—people who are temporary residents while passing through.

Perhaps you have traveled to, or been a temporary resident in, a foreign country. You may have been advised of precautions to take while in that country. Perhaps dietary cautions were in order. Or perhaps you needed to be advised of certain laws in that country. Or you may have needed to be advised of rules governing travel. Or you may have been advised about customs or the personal sensibilities of the people among whom you would be for a time. Such advisories are helpful and may even be crucial for a safe and successful visit.

Hebrews is a letter written to advise and encourage Christians, who know they are "aliens and strangers on earth" on their way to "a better country—a heavenly one" (Hebrews 11:13, 16).

B. Hebrews Is a Word of Encouragement

At an unidentified time and place in the first century A.D., a particular group of Christian pilgrims needed this travel advisory; in fact, they were in serious danger. They were in danger of losing the true faith. So God put it into the heart and mind of a Christian teacher to send them a "word of exhortation" (Hebrews 13:22).

Who was this teacher? Some have suggested Paul, but this is not likely for a number of reasons we cannot discuss now. Perhaps it was Apollos or Barnabas or another of Paul's associates. It was written either from Rome or to Rome (Hebrews 13:24). But we do not know for sure. The fact is, the name of the author and identity of those first readers have been long forgotten. But God's inspired words in the Epistle to the Hebrews have encouraged pilgrims for centuries ever since.

May this study help you understand and receive that word of encouragement so that your faith is strengthened and your endurance is increased, resulting in your being brought to that heavenly home!

C. The Message and Plan of Hebrews—Boiled Down

The author wrote to a specific audience. He wanted them to do certain things. And he told them why they should do it, always backing up his reasons with passages from the Old Testament Scriptures. Approaching Hebrews in this way, we find three simple and memorable commands in Hebrews: (1) *Listen;* (2) *draw near;* (3) *endure. Listen* to the Word of God revealed through the Son, Jesus (1:1–4:13). *Draw near* to God through the High Priest, Jesus (4:14–10:22). *Endure* through faith, which looks up to Jesus (10:23–13:35).

This is the essence of this word of encouragement.

2 Listen to the Son

A. He Reveals God (1:1–4)

The very first sentence of Hebrews (1:1–2) tells us that these days, since Jesus has appeared, are the Last Days. With Jesus' coming, the writer asserts, God's way of speaking has changed. In former times God spoke through prophets. But now, in these Last Days, He has spoken to us by His Son, Jesus. The writer refers to Jesus' person and work with a series of seven concise statements (vv. 2–4). He declares, concerning Jesus: (1) He is appointed heir of all things (at the end); (2) He was God's agent of creation (at the beginning); (3) He is the radiance of God's glory and the imprint-copy of God's being; (4) He upholds the universe by His powerful command; (5) He provided purification for our sins; (6) He sat down at the right hand of God in heaven; (7) He has received a name and inheritance better than the angels.

With these declarations the writer begins a major point: Jesus, and the new covenant He brought into being, is superior. What we have in Christ is better—far better! Even the disgrace and possible persecution we may be called on to bear for the sake of Christ does not diminish the superiority of Christ and of the covenant that came about through Him. The writer will speak of this superiority throughout this letter.

B. He Is Superior to Angels (1:5–14)

The seventh assertion—that Christ is superior to angels—leads to the next section, where the writer marshals Old Testament passages to tell of the superiority of this exalted and enthroned Son over the angels. This demonstration is important for two reasons. First, some Jews held that various angels were closer to God and more powerful than the Messiah, whom they held to be only a human king (Son of David). Hebrews proves that Christ, the Son of David, who became a human being and made purification for sins, is also truly the Son of God. While Christ humbled Himself and "was made a little lower than the angels" (2:9) for a time, He has now been exalted far above all angels. Second, God made use of angels in connection with His revelation of the Law in the Old Testament. Hebrews 2:2; Galatians 3:19; and Acts 7:53 all indicate that angels were involved in the giving of the Law at Mount Sinai. Therefore, the Word of God spoken of old was through prophets and associated with angels. But a message brought through angels can never be set above the Gospel revealed in Jesus. Nor is any angel the ruler of the world to come. No, angels are ministering spirits, God's servants appointed for the sake of people who are to be saved (1:14).

The author makes this point that Christ is superior to angels with a long string of Old Testament passages and a concluding summary of his own (v. 14). He quotes verses (mostly from the psalms) that speak of the Messiah, the Son of David and the Son of God. These passages show that the Son (1) is begotten by God (v. 5); (2) is worshiped by the angels (v. 6); (3) is an eternal and upright king (vv. 7–8); (4) is anointed by God to be above all others (v. 9); (5) is eternal and unchanging (vv. 10–12); (6) has been commanded to sit at God's right hand (v. 13). Two prominent psalm verses, 2:7 and 110:1, open and close the chain, testifying to the enthronement of the Messiah. Throughout this collection of Bible passages the angels are shown to be subservient to the Son: they worship Him (v. 6) and are winds or spirits, flickering flames of fire (v. 7). Hebrews concludes (v. 14) that God has created angels to be ministering spirits to help people who are to be saved, not dominating powers to be feared and served by humans.

Angels serve as agents of God's care of us, His people. This is great comfort and reassurance for us. God's holy angels watch over and guard us, both in spiritual and in physical matters. These invisible servants of God, who surround us every moment, are another evidence that our God loves us and preserves us in all our ways. How grateful we can be to God for the service of the angels, creatures of our God as we are, who obediently serve God by watching over and caring for us. Though holy and more powerful than we, the angels serve us as they carry out God's will in regard to us.

C. He Must Therefore Be Heard (2:1–4)

Now we come to a paragraph of encouragement. The basis of this encouragement is what has just been asserted and proven in chapter 1. Since the Son is above the angels, the word He spoke should be listened to even more keenly than the revelation given through the angels (i.e., the Law at Mount Sinai). This does not mean that the Old Testament is to be rejected. The Old

Testament is God's Word and is to be heeded. But its meaning and purpose is to be seen in the light of the revelation in Jesus, not the other way around. The Gospel, testified to in the Old Testament but revealed in all its clarity in Jesus, is God's final word and is to be heeded most carefully. The content of that Gospel is alluded to in 1:3 ("after He had provided purification for sins") and will be stated more explicitly soon (see 2:9: "that . . . He might taste death for everyone").

Here, in verses 3–4, we have a description of how that revelation of salvation has been preserved for us. First, (v. 3) it was spoken by the Lord; then those who heard Him confirmed it to us.

How can we be sure that they delivered the truth of the Gospel to us? God Himself testified to the truth of their preaching with signs, wonders, various miracles, and special gifts of the Holy Spirit. The miracles performed by the apostles were God's seal of approval on the content of their preaching.

The apostles and eyewitnesses of Jesus at first delivered His Gospel in oral preaching and teaching. As time went by, they were inspired to write their reports, their witness, and their teaching in the Gospels and in their Epistles. In this way the Holy Scripture of the New Testament, the divinely confirmed apostolic testimony, comes to us, and we receive the true Gospel, the Word of our Lord, the Son of God.

How wonderfully God has given and preserved for us the Gospel witness by way of the divinely inspired Scriptures! How we ought to treasure and make daily use of the Bible! The Bible is, as one hymn says, like a jewel case made of gold, in which we find the sparkling gem of the Holy Gospel, by which we are saved!

D. The Old Testament Points to Him as the Coming King (2:5–18)

Angels are not to be the powerful rulers of the world to come. Jesus Christ, Son of God and Son of David, true God and true man, has that honor. Jesus, who made purification for sin through His incarnation and death, has been exalted to rule forever. Precisely that God-man Jesus, who suffered and died, is the captain of our salvation, the eternal King who came to rescue the lost.

And the Old Testament testifies to this. Hebrews (2:6–7) introduces verses from Psalm 8 that find their fulfillment and complete meaning in Jesus. That psalm says, "You made him [the son of man] a little lower than the angels." But the phrase "a little" can mean either "a little bit" or "a little while." Hebrews shows us that the verse finds its fulfillment in Jesus (2:8), who for a little while (when He humbled Himself to become a man so He might give His life for us) was lower than the angels (v. 9). His purpose in lowering Himself in this way was that He might die, tasting death in the place of everyone, and then be crowned with glory and honor by God in the events following His death on the cross. Jesus' becoming a man for the purpose of becoming our substitute before God is the key to understanding Psalm 8!

Hebrews 2:10 pictures Jesus as a leader (captain of salvation) bringing many to the glorious goal; it was God's plan to bring Him to the goal ("make . . . perfect") through suffering. "To perfect" in Hebrews means "to bring to the goal." Jesus, as the Savior of mankind, is (v. 11) "of the same family" of those He came to save, our "brother."

To show the Old Testament basis for this (in vv. 12–13), the writer cites Psalm 22 and Isaiah 8. He became a man so He might die and, by dying, defeat and destroy the devil and set all people free from the fear of death. His incarnation (becoming man) was necessary, because those He came to save are not the angels but human beings ("Abraham's descendants," that is, believers). And to accomplish this purpose to do away with sin as our Substitute and to help us in our need—He had to become like us in every way. He had to become one of us.

We can only bow in wonder and thanksgiving as we review this wonderful truth. God Himself came down to us in Jesus to save us by lifting us out of our sins to Himself in glory! What gracious love stands behind God's coming into this world in Jesus! May that amazing, divine love move us to respond with gratitude and praise as we give Jesus our worship, obedience, and service!

3 Review of the Main Points

A. The Encouragement

Now let's review what God has told us in this section from Hebrews. We have seen how the Word of God came in three time periods: (1) of old through the prophets and angels; (2) by the Lord, God's Son, in these Last Days; and (3) "today," when it is preached and spoken to the current generation by those who have received it from those who heard the Lord. The Word revealed of old through prophets and angels, which we now call the Old Testament, was divine, powerful, and to be taken seriously. It challenged the hearers to believe, and it discerned and punished unbelief (2:2; 4:12). Since that is true, we ought to take the Word revealed through the Son of God with utmost seriousness: to neglect the salvation it offers is to lose everything. So this is the first chief encouragement, as summarized in 2:1: to pay even closer heed to the Gospel, the Word of Jesus.

B. Doctrinal Rationale, Based on Scripture

Jesus is the final and perfect revealer of God, greater than angels and greater than the greatest prophet, Moses. As true God and true man, Jesus is the one perfect mediator between God and mankind. St. John taught the same thing when he described, at the beginning of his Gospel, how (John 1:14, 18) "the Word became flesh" and how "the One and Only, who is at the Father's side, has made Him known." That God's Son, Jesus, is greater than the angels is stated in the Old Testament Scripture (Hebrews 1:5–13). That Jesus was also true man and so able to help and to die for His brothers is also proved from Old Testament Scripture (Hebrews 2:6–18). This is the Son who has been exalted to rule forever.

C. The Decisive Assertion of Superiority

Since Jesus Himself is superior, His Word is superior. The Word of God came also through angels and prophets. But the key and controlling revelation, the highest and clearest, is the Son Himself, begotten of the Father from all eternity, born of the Virgin Mary, died, raised, and exalted forever. Jesus was God incarnate. Jesus revealed and taught the complete truth. Some who heard Him gave a solemn account of it for us—an account whose truthfulness God Himself confirmed by granting to those first-generation eyewitnesses, evangelists, and apostles (2:4) "signs, wonders and various miracles, and gifts of the Holy Spirit distributed according to His will." The Word before Jesus, the Old Testament, meant nothing other than what Jesus Himself revealed. He is the fulfillment and so also is the key for understanding the Old Testament. All who do not find the Old Testament fulfilled in Jesus are bound to get the Old Testament wrong. (John 5:39) "You diligently study the Scriptures," Jesus told the Jews, "because you think that by them you possess eternal life. These are the Scriptures that testify about Me."

The Word today, proclaimed by the church, must never be anything other than what Jesus revealed and what the divinely appointed and attested apostles and evangelists handed on to us. The Word of God in Jesus delivered to us in the inspired Scriptures of the New Testament is the final authority and judge of all preaching and teaching in the church. (John 8:31) "If you hold to My teaching," Jesus said, "you are really My disciples."

D. Implications for Today

So we can also judge contemporary preachers and rightly interpret the words of the Old Testament prophets by noting how they do or do not coincide with the Gospel revealed in Jesus. (Matthew 17:5) "This is My Son, whom I love," said the voice from the cloud. "Listen to Him!" The author of Hebrews is saying the same thing. Christians now can "listen to Him" by studying the inspired writings of the evangelists and apostles of the New Testament. Preachers devoted to preaching nothing else and who teach and interpret the Old Testament as testimony to Jesus are faithful voices. They call and guide and help weary pilgrims to persevere on the journey of faith. They let the Word of God in Jesus be (Psalm 119:105) the light to our path and the lamp to our feet.

Concluding Activities

Make any necessary announcements and distribute study leaflet 2 and the enrichment magazine. Encourage participants to browse in the magazine and keep it as a helpful reference for coming lessons.

Encourage participants to set a weekly plan for their LifeLight study. A consistent daily schedule works best for most. Some begin or end the day with LifeLight. Others find another time during the day at home or during lunch hours at work. Invite participants to share their practices, especially if your group has some who are new to LifeLight.

Listen Today and Believe

Hebrews 3:1–4:13

Preparing for the Session

Central Focus

The Word of God addresses us today; hearing it with faith leads to our entering the promised eternal rest.

Objectives

That participants, led by the Holy Spirit, will

1. understand the Spirit's warning to listen to the Gospel now in this "today" of opportunity;
2. earnestly yearn to enter the heavenly rest;
3. believe more firmly the Gospel message;
4. hear and heed the Gospel Word by weekly worship, daily Bible reading, and faithful study of the Bible with fellow Christians.

Note for the small-group leaders: Lesson notes and other materials you will need begin on page 00.

For the Lecture Leader

Bible Background

Materials from several Old Testament passages hover in the background of this section. It is wise to review them and highlight their import.

1. Genesis 2:2 states that on the seventh day God rested from all the work He had done. This established a pattern in which there is revealed a prophecy and promise: six days of work in the life of this age and rest on the seventh, when no work of this world is to be done. To testify to that pattern and that otherworldly rest, God commanded the Israelites to rest every seventh day of the week. When Jesus came, He brought a new era, the promised kingdom of God, heavenly rest and peace. Since Jesus has come as our Savior and Lord, God no longer requires us to observe the Sabbath day and other holy days of the Old Testament (Colossians 2:16–17). But God does require Christians to worship together (Acts 2:42, 46; Hebrews 10:25). The church worships together especially on Sunday, because Christ rose from the dead on Sunday (Luke 24:1–2; Acts 20:7).

2. God had the Promised Land of Canaan prepared and waiting for those who left Egypt with Moses. But they showed lack of trust in God by their faultfinding and murmuring at Massah and Meribah (Exodus 17:1–7; Psalm 95:8–9; Hebrews 3:8–9). Because of such unbelief, they wandered 40 years in the wilderness. A whole generation (except for Joshua and Caleb) died off there and did not make it to the Promised Land of Canaan. That failure to believe and failure to attain the goal is a pattern recorded to warn future generations.

3. In the time of David that word of God's reign and that warning not to reject it with the hardened heart of unbelief were repeated in Psalm 95. The important thing to note here is the oath (Psalm 95:11; Hebrews 3:11) and the word *today* (3:7). God has a rest. It was offered to some, but they did not enter it. Years later, in the time of David, the appeal was again given to hear His voice and respond not with unfaith but with faith. The implication is that the "rest" offered is not in this world's history but at the end of this world's history. It was not accomplished when Joshua defeated all the Canaanites (Hebrews 4:8). Nor was it accomplished when David conquered all of his enemies. Nor is it even accomplished yet, for the Son of David, Jesus Christ, has been told: "Sit at My right hand until I make Your enemies a footstool for Your feet" (Psalm 110:1). Thus "there remains, then, a Sabbath-rest for the people of God" (Hebrews 4:9)—the rest prophesied at creation and foreshadowed in the Sabbath of the Old Testament. And the Word of God, living and active, still addresses people *today*, in the day of the author of Hebrews and in our day, so long as this world's history continues.

Session Plan

Worship

Begin the session with the hymn printed in the study leaflet. Accompaniments are available in denominational hymnals, such as *Lutheran Worship* (refer to hymnal index). Note: Concordia Publishing House has available *Every Voice a Song*, a 9-CD set of organ accompaniments for 180 hymns and liturgy. All the initial worship hymns in the LifeLight courses are included in this resource. It's especially helpful for mission congregations and small parishes. See the list of study resources on page 00.

Devotion

Perhaps you are familiar with the adage that tells us "opportunity knocks but once." There are many opportunities that do seem to come once and must be accepted then. Such an opportunity may not come again.

God is presenting us with an opportunity—the opportunity to hear and believe the Gospel and, in doing so, to be saved. God, in His mercy and grace, usually offers this opportunity not once but many times, perhaps countless times in a lifetime. But we never know when the opportunity we have to hear and believe the Gospel will be the last such opportunity. Finally, there will come a day when such an opportunity, though not the first, is the last. The opportunity will not come again.

Therefore the urgent plea: "*Today*, if you hear His voice, do not harden your hearts" (Hebrews 3:7–8, quoting Psalm 95:7–8). Or, in the words of Paul: "I tell you, now is the time of God's favor, *now* is the day of salvation" (2 Corinthians 6:2). We cannot assume that there will come another time to believe the Gospel or that there is no particular hurry to accept God's invitation. Each time we hear the Gospel we may say to ourselves: "This may be it. This may be the last opportunity that will be given me. Now is the time to believe."

Listen *today* and believe!

Pray together the prayer printed in the study leaflet.

Lecture Presentation

1 Introduction

A. Linking This Segment to the Preceding Section

To begin the lecture use an attention-getting device: a whistle, a loud "Listen up!" or a sharp clap of the hands might do the job.

Did you ever have to get the attention of a group in that way? You probably have if you have ever been a scout leader, a parent with several children, or a LifeLight lecturer—just kidding.

But the author of the letter to the Hebrews isn't kidding as he says to us, "Listen to the Son—*now*!—and believe."

In the section we studied last week the author emphasized the need to listen to the Word revealed in the Son even more attentively than to the Old Testament Word alone. The section we studied this week tells us about the nature of the Word of God and the manner of listening required for it to work beneficially for the hearer.

Sometimes we may have the idea that the written word is a lifeless thing. That is not true, of course, as anyone who enjoys reading knows. And it certainly is not true of God's Word! As long as this world stands, God's Word is and will be living, active, challenging, and judging. God's Word says, "Listen *today!*" as it addresses each subsequent generation.

B. Key Concepts in Hebrews 3:7–4:13

As we work through these paragraphs, we find several important themes. We need to have these themes clear in our minds. The most important theme is the contrast between hearing with an evil, hardened heart and hearing with faith (Hebrews 3:12–13; 4:2).

We are confronted with a mystery here. The Holy Spirit enables some to know the secret of the Kingdom. They hear rightly and believe and understand. Their hearing is a hearing by faith, a faith produced in the hearing itself (Romans 10:17).

On the other hand, hearing God's Word has just the opposite effect in others. Consider the generation of Israelites whom God led out of Egypt. Though they heard the Word, they heard it with unbelief, with hearts hardened against the Word they were hearing. They did not receive God's Word with faith.

We need to receive the true Word of God as it comes from outside us with trusting, accepting faith in order to enter God's rest (salvation). This is the first important theme in this section.

And that leads us to the second important theme, that of the Sabbath-rest (Hebrews 4:1–5). What is this Sabbath-rest? Entering the Promised Land and the command to do no work on the seventh day testified to this rest. The Sabbath-rest, is the end-time rest of heaven, the kingdom of God. Entering the Promised Land and doing no work on the seventh day both pointed to this.

The third important theme is "Today" (Hebrews 4:6–13). The Word of God addresses each generation in its own day and invites it to receive salvation through faith. Since the promised rest comes at the end of this world's history, the Word that promises the rest and calls for and calls forth faith is present, relevant, and addressed to every generation, (Hebrews 3:13) "as long as it is called Today," until the end of the age comes.

Hearing with faith; Sabbath-rest; the Word today, living, active, and effective these are the themes in Hebrews 3:7–4:13. Let's recognize that these themes are also addressed to us.

2 Listen Today and Believe

A. Beware of Hardening Your Heart (3:7–15)

With this overview of the major themes in mind, let's go back to the beginning of this section once again. The previous verse, Hebrews 3:6, introduces the idea of persevering and anticipates the third great encouragement to endure. Holding on to our courage and hope calls for paying careful attention to the Gospel. Now our author moves on to encourage the right and fruitful kind of listening by calling up Old Testament passages that warn us against hearing with a hard or unbelieving heart.

Our author cites Psalm 95:7–11. The passage refers to the entire 40-year period during which the Israelites were led through the desert to the Promised Land. During this entire period the Israelites provoked the Lord with their repeated complaining and faithlessness. However, two incidents receive special attention. The first is recorded in Exodus 17:1–7, where the Israelites complained of thirst. In response, the Lord commanded Moses to strike a rock, and water gushed from it. The names *Massah* (meaning "testing") and *Meribah* (meaning "quarreling") were given to the place after the sins the Israelites had committed there. The Hebrew text of Psalm 95 retains these names; the Greek text of the psalm cited by the author of Hebrews refers to what the names mean: "rebellion" and "testing."

The second incident from the exodus is reported in Numbers 13, where scouts are sent into the Promised Land. They returned to report that the land was good and fruitful, but 10 of the 12 scouts advised not entering the land. They maintained that the land's present inhabitants would be too strong for the Israelites. Only Caleb and Joshua expressed confidence that the Lord would keep His promises to give them the land. The Lord responded to this refusal to believe His promises and to obey His command to enter the land. He swore that none of that generation of Israelites except Caleb and Joshua would enter the Promised Land. Only their children would enter it. The Israelites of that generation were condemned to be shut out of the land in which the Lord would give Israel rest.

B. Learn from the Unbelief of Ancient Israel (3:16–19)

God brought a generation of Israelites out of Egypt under the leadership of Moses. The Lord rescued them and protected and provided for them as they made their way across the desert. They had seen many miracles and had heard the Lord's promise that He was bringing them to a land of rest and peace. And yet they did not enter that land of rest. Why not? Was it God's fault? Certainly not! Did they hear the Word? Yes, they did. Why, then, did they not enter? Because they failed to trust God and to obey Him.

Two terms express their failure: (v. 19) *unbelief*, a failure to trust; and (v. 18) *disobedience*, a failure to be convinced and to act accordingly. Though distinct, those two ideas are always linked: faith and obedience. Behind all disobedient, rebellious behavior lies unbelief. The account of the Israelites during the exodus and the commentary on that account in Psalm 95 reveal this instructive fact: (3:19) "They were not able to enter, because of their unbelief."

Is it possible that a serious warning is meant for us also in this earnest admonition? Is it possible for us who have received the Holy Spirit in Word and Sacraments to yet reject Him? Is it possible for us who have the Gospel to fail to receive it with faith? Is it possible for our hearts to grow cold with unbelief? Is it possible that the devil may find an unguarded entrance into our hearts and gradually take them over? Is it possible, with all of our advantages, that such an end might still come upon us?

Certainly our own experience bears out what we learn in this Bible passage. When our faith in God is strongest and most alive, we find it easier to resist temptations to disobey God. But when we fail to keep our faith strong and well nourished, then we find we are most prone to disobey God and to sin against Him. The conclusion is obvious. If we would obey God we must give the Holy Spirit plenty of opportunities to nourish and strengthen our faith as we pay attention to the Gospel and incorporate God's Word and Sacraments into our weekly living.

C. Turn in Faith to the Promised Rest (4:1–2)

Three points are made, as the Israelites of the exodus are compared with the present readers: (1) the promise of entering God's rest still remains; (2) just as those Israelites heard the Good News preached to them, so do we; and (3) (v. 2) "the message they heard was of no value to them, because those who heard did not combine it with faith." If it happened before, it can happen again, and that is just what the author of Hebrews is afraid of. This warning is of the greatest importance for understanding the whole section.

D. We Shall Enter That Rest! (4:3–11)

Verse 3 begins with a straightforward statement: "Now we who have believed enter [are going to enter] that rest." Then our author proceeds to show from the Old Testament how that must be true. The argument follows these steps: (1) In the time of the kings (Psalm 95) God said He had sworn that certain (earlier) people would not enter His rest. (2) But (vv. 3b–4) God had finished with all of His work after the six days of creation and rested on the seventh day. (3) (V. 6) So there was from creation some kind of rest of God waiting for people to enter into it. (4) (V. 6b) The ones who formerly had the Good News spoken to them did not enter into that rest because of disobedience. (5) (Vv. 6–8) When God spoke of another rest, available "today" in the days of the kings, that showed that the rest in Canaan under Joshua was not the real rest. (6) (V. 9) Therefore, there is still a great Sabbath-rest waiting for the people of God. (7) Those who enter it rest from their works in this world, as God did. This shows that the rest in store for us is the eternal life in heaven in the age that will come when this present life, with its burdens and troubles, is past.

The "rest" spoken of is not something that will happen in this world, like entering into Canaan. It is a heavenly rest, a rest that takes place in another world. Genesis 2:2 shows that God's rest has lasted since the end of creation and suggests that observing the Sabbath was to be an anticipation of the eternal, heavenly rest. Psalm 95:7–11 tells us how we enter into that rest: by hearing God's Word "today" without a hardened heart. The "rest" is heavenly. And hearing the Good News with faith is the key that opens the door to that rest.

E. God's Word Does God's Work (4:12–13)

Fittingly, the section that encourages hearers to listen with faith (4:12–13) concludes with one of Scripture's most memorable statements about the Word of God. Whenever and wherever it is preached—in all the "todays" from the start of creation to the end of this world—it is living, powerful, and active. That is the Word we are dealing with—or, rather, that deals with us! It cuts into all who hear it and lays bare their souls, whether they are believers, those who trust in God, or unbelievers. It exposes and condemns unbelievers just as surely as it rescues and protects believers. And so it divides all hearers into two groups: believers and unbelievers, the ones being saved and the ones rejecting the gift of salvation.

Thank God that the Spirit has used that Word to bring us to repentance and faith! Pray God that He will use our sharing of that living and active Word to confront and bring many others to repentance and faith!

3 Review of the Main Points

A. The Encouragement

Now let's review the main points of our study this week. Our author knows and points to where the Word of truth is: it is spoken in Jesus, the Son. What reception will the Word meet? Our author earnestly warns against hearing with a hard heart; he encourages receiving the Good News with faith, with a trusting and believing and obeying heart.

B. The Biblical Basis for the Encouragement

This encouragement rests on some careful reading of three sections of Scripture. Genesis 2:2 and Psalm 95:8–10 (which recounts Exodus 17) tell us that the rest offered to us will take place in heaven, not on this earth. They earnestly urge us to hear God's Word with faith. They describe God's Word to us as alive and active, exposing belief and unbelief and dividing all those who hear it into believers and unbelievers. Scripture underlines the urgency of receiving this Word now, "Today," when the opportunity is still ours.

4 Implications for Today

A. The Sword of the Word

Like the Israelites of the exodus and the first readers of Hebrews, we also have had the Good News proclaimed to us. And hearing that Good News is a lot different from hearing the evening news on TV. You can switch off the TV news and not be the worse for it. But when the Gospel of God's work in Jesus Christ is proclaimed, everyone who hears it is put in a crucial position. Jesus said of those who had heard the Gospel but had rejected it that a "verdict" had been reached in their case. He explained, (John 3:18) "Whoever believes in Him is not condemned, but whoever does not believe stands condemned already because he has not believed in the name of God's one and only Son." The Word of God is always active and effective. If it is not saving, it is condemning. There is no neutral ground with the Gospel.

B. Faith Alone

The first section of Hebrews taught Christ alone and Scripture alone; this section teaches faith alone. The Word of truth is out there. But faith is necessary to receive the benefit of the Word, the eventual entrance into the heavenly rest. Where does that faith originate? Faith comes from hearing the Word of God.

By nature all hearts are hard and dull. In some—and it is a mystery why in some and not in others—the power of God overcomes the hardness and creates faith. It is also true that Christian persons, baptized believers, can resist the Holy Spirit, harden their hearts, and lose their faith. This, too, is a mystery and a tragedy. It happens as a result of the deceit of sin and long neglect of the means of grace.

How can we be sure it's not happening to us? First, we must know that it can happen, so that we do not become complacent. Second, we can pray to be kept in the faith. And third, we can continue to listen to the Word, fixing our eyes on Jesus, the source of all our strength. In that way we are kept safe through the trials and temptations we meet in this world until we reach our heavenly home.

C. The Heavenly Rest

In our study this week we have learned the true meaning of the Sabbath-rest. The command to rest on the seventh day of the week was based on God's resting after six days of creating the universe. Sabbath-keeping was meant to teach and remind the Israelites that there is another world, the kingdom of God.

What the Jewish Sabbath pointed forward to arrived in Jesus. Christians enter that life of the new age. All time and all godly callings are sanctified as we worship God and offer our whole selves as living sacrifices. No longer are we bound to observe the ceremonial laws of the Old Testament that pointed ahead to the coming of the Savior. For the Savior has come. We gather together on Sundays and at other times to listen to the Son and so be strengthened and preserved in faith and brought to the pilgrim's goal, heavenly rest.

Closing Activities

Make any necessary announcements and distribute study leaflet 3. Ask whether participants are enjoying the enrichment magazine.

Our Great High Priest

Hebrews 4:14–6:20

Preparing for the Session

Central Focus

Draw near to God through Jesus, our High Priest, who has undergone suffering and death and has ascended and entered the heavenly temple.

Objectives

That participants, led by the Holy Spirit, will

1. understand how and why Jesus is our great High Priest;
2. desire to draw nearer to Jesus through faith;
3. be ready for solid food, that is, for a more mature understanding of God's Word concerning Jesus;
4. publicly confess Jesus as their Savior;
5. rely on Jesus as the anchor of their hope concerning God;
6. resolve to follow Jesus to the goal—the rest God has prepared for His people in heaven.

Note for the small-group leaders: Lesson notes and other materials you will need begin on page 00.

For the Lecture Leader

Bible Background

As the topic shifts from words of revelation to deeds of salvation, the main points of comparison become the appointment and actions of Aaron and the Old Testament priests, on the one hand, and the earthly ministry, death, and ascension of Jesus' priestly work on the other. It is especially important at this point to review what the Old Testament has to say about the high priest, especially about his movements and actions on Yom Kippur, the great Day of Atonement (Leviticus 16). The special calling and privilege of this divinely instituted office bearer should not be missed. Though the high priest is a man of sinful flesh himself, he is allowed, by God's command, to make sacrifice for himself and so be sanctified and consecrated. He becomes, by grace, an appointed mediator to approach the holy God on behalf of sinful people. By God's call and direction, the institution of the high priesthood was the final plank in a bridge over the gap between the holy God and the fallen, sinful world.

Picture it this way: when sin came, a chasm opened between the holy God and the sinful world. God would send His Son to cross that chasm and bridge that gap. To prophesy of and to prepare for the salvation He would provide, God called Israel, out of all the nations, to be "His" holy people. They were not sinless, but they were called to be a place of God's revelation and preparation for Jesus. In building a bridge between the sinful world and the holy God, they were a first plank in the revelation model. The true Israel was Christ. And within Israel, the Levites were a second plank, set aside for God. And within the Levites, the priests. And from within the priests, the high priest—a foreshadowing of the sinless mediator God would send. For the sake of revealing that grace of God in Jesus—and only for that sake—Israel was called, the Levitical order of priesthood was instituted, and the ritual of Yom Kippur was commanded.

The second element of Bible background to this lesson is from the New Testament Gospels, where Jesus' birth and Baptism (Jesus' installation into His office by God) are reported, where His prayers and intercessions are recorded, where His obedient suffering and death are described, and where His resurrection and ascension to God's throne in heaven are revealed. These are all connected to the priestly pattern of office and work.

Jesus is an apostle *to* us and a priest *for* us (Session 2). More to the point, Jesus is our High Priest, our *great* High Priest. There are elements about Him that make Him special and unique, our High Priest above and beyond any other priest.

Session Plan

Worship

Begin the session with the hymn printed in the study leaflet. Accompaniments are available in denominational hymnals, such as *Lutheran Worship* (refer to hymnal index). Note: Concordia Publishing House has available *Every Voice a Song,* a 9-CD set of organ accompaniments for 180 hymns and liturgy. All the initial worship hymns in the LifeLight courses are included in this resource. It's especially helpful for mission congregations and small parishes. See the list of study resources on page 00.

Devotion

What makes a person a hero?

We might say two qualities cause someone to become a hero. First, the person who becomes a hero is someone with whom we can identify. He or she is someone who is, in most respects, like us. A hero is someone we admire and aspire to be like. That means that person must be someone we can be like.

The other quality that makes someone a hero is that he or she has done something truly extraordinary, something admirable, something that shows great courage, self-sacrifice, and other qualities to a remarkable degree. That is what makes the person heroic.

In the section we studied this week the author of Hebrews presents Jesus as our great High Priest. As our High Priest, Jesus became one of us, a real human being, one who shares our situation. But also as our High Priest, Jesus did something on our behalf, something extraordinary and remarkable, something beyond what we do or can do. He offered Himself as the sacrifice of atonement for our sins. No further sacrifice is needed to atone for our sins, because Jesus has done it all!

What a hero! More than a hero—what a High Priest we have in Jesus! Let us praise and adore Him!

Pray together the prayer printed in the study leaflet.

Lecture Presentation

1 Introduction of Issues

Do you hold an office of some kind? You may have been elected or appointed to some office, perhaps secretary or treasurer of some organization. That usually means a little honor and a lot of work.

One of the ways in which we discuss the ministry of Jesus is by arranging His work under three descriptive categories called "offices." These are the offices of prophet, priest, and king. Perhaps the least understood of these is "priest." Most of us are not familiar with priests of the sort that were common in Old Testament times. Priests were set apart from ordinary folk and their ordinary lives. Priests lived by higher, stricter rules, had special vestments, were set apart (consecrated), and had to worry about their special cleanness or fitness to serve. They presided over the offerings and sacrifices in the temple, spoke prayers, and pronounced, taught, and interpreted the Law.

We all know and remember easily enough that Jesus, the Lamb of God, died as our substitute and so was a sacrificial victim. But, as a hymn phrase expresses, He was "Himself the victim and Himself the priest." We are less accustomed to think of Jesus' ministry as the work of a priest. But, in fact, He was a priest. Actually, every office and institution in the Old Testament was meant to point forward to Him and to be fulfilled in Him. This includes the office and ministry of the Old Testament priests.

The author of Hebrews invites us to be ready for some "meaty stuff" in this section—something for which every good student is always eager.

2 Our Great High Priest

Our author encourages us to (4:14) "hold firmly to the faith we profess" and to (4:16) "approach the throne of grace with confidence." What is the Bible basis for this encouragement? We have a High Priest, Jesus the Son of God, who has passed through the skies to God's presence and yet who also can sympathize with us and help us. We are to draw near so that we might receive mercy and find help.

(5:1–4) First, the writer refers to some characteristics of a typical high priest. (1) (V. la) He is taken from among his peers so he might represent them in matters related to God and in this way do some good for those from whom he came. (2) (V. 1b) He offers gifts and sacrifices for sins. (3) (V. 2a) He is able to deal gently with the ignorant and the wandering, because he is made of the same stuff they are. (4) (V. 2b) Since this is so, he must make offerings for his own sins just as he does for those he serves. (5) And finally, verse 4 emphasizes again what was implied in the passive voice of verse 1: He is called and appointed to his priestly office; he does not take it by himself.

(5:5–10) Similarly, (1) (v. 5a) Jesus did not take this office upon Himself, but He was called and appointed to it by God the Father. (Vv. 5b–6) This truth is proved by quoting verses from two messianic psalms, 2:7 and 110:4. (2) (V. 7) Jesus, the Son of God, became man and, as the God-man Messiah, made intercessions and prayers to God. God raised Him from the dead (saved Him from death), proving that Jesus' sacrifice was acceptable to God. God heard Him, and God only hears the righteous, the ones in a right relationship to Him. (3) (V. 8) Even though He was true God and God's Son, as true man He submitted to the discipline of learning obedience through suffering. (4) (V. 9) He has become the source of eternal salvation for all those believing and obeying Him. (5) (V. 10) He was brought through to the goal: raised, ascended, and exalted to sit and reign forever at God's right hand.

At this point (5:6) our author mentions Melchizedek, an Old Testament figure who will be discussed rather extensively in our next lesson. Melchizedek was an Old Testament priest/king who pointed ahead to Christ.

But now back to our author's discussion of Christ as High Priest. (5:11–14) The writer tells the Hebrews: If we are to explain to you how this teaching of the High Priesthood of the Messiah comes from the Old Testament, we must first challenge you to grow up in your understanding of the Bible. You are going to have to move from infancy toward maturity as regards the Word of righteousness, from milk to solid food. You should be teachers by now, but, actually, you are still at the level of children, unskilled with the Word of righteousness.

The way to grow toward this maturity is through practice. You must exercise those faculties that will enable you to discriminate between that which is noble, worthwhile, and virtuous and that which is vain, empty, worthless, and evil. By engaging in this form of exercise, these faculties will develop as they should. Such a development is necessary if you are to build a virtuous Christian character, one familiar with and skilled in the Word of righteousness, one that reacts by habit, automatically, to every situation, according to God's revelation and will.

We all know the value of practice in many areas of life, such as in athletics, music, and public speaking. The examples are endless. Do we know that practice is also important in developing our spiritual life? Do we know the importance of Bible study—I mean real study, study that is challenging, that stretches us? I know that you do know the value of challenging Bible study. That is why you are in this LifeLight course.

The writer of Hebrews continues in 6:1–4: Therefore, God willing, we are going to go beyond the elementary teachings about the Messiah and move on toward more mature teaching. We will assume that, in your case, the foundation has been adequately laid and that you are able to follow, if you are willing.

How important that we understand the basis for this encouragement not to fall away from faith in Christ but to continue to grow in Him. There is a frightful end in store for those who hear the Good News again and again but do not believe in Jesus and by following Him. Those who believed in Jesus but then fall away and repudiate Jesus, the crucified Messiah, have no alternative means to repent and be saved. In rejecting Jesus such people are (v. 6) "crucifying the Son of God all over again"; they are repeating the same act of rejecting Jesus as those who actually nailed Him to the cross.

So long as they continue to crucify God's Son "all over again" and to subject Him to "public disgrace" by denying Him in whom they once believed, they cannot find a new way to repent and be saved. Of course, the moment they stop crucifying Jesus anew—as soon as they repent and put their trust in Him once again—they will be forgiven. The eagerness of God to receive back repentant sinners is illustrated in Jesus' memorable parable of the prodigal, or lost, son in Luke 15:11–32.

The point of verses 4–6 is to warn wavering Christians

not to persist in a refusal to acknowledge faith in Jesus, in a failure to draw near to God through Him. This would be absolutely the wrong response to the Word revealed from heaven. The short parable of verses 7–8 makes that clear. Rain comes down from God in heaven. The earth drinks it in, receives it. If the land produces plants useful to those for whose sake it is cultivated, all is well and the land is blessed. But should the land produce thorns and thistles, that would make the land worthless and put it under a curse (see Genesis 3:17). The end result is not a blessing from God, but the fire!

Now for the point of that parable. The Word of the Gospel is like the rain. The hearers on whom the Gospel Word falls are like the earth. If the hearers respond (acknowledging Jesus with faith, drawing near to God through Jesus), the end result is blessing. If the hearers reject Jesus and spurn the Gospel, there can be only one result: the curse and fire of hell!

What a frightening prospect! (6:9–12) But, the writer assures the Hebrews, we are confident of a better prospect in your case. You have shown in the past, and are now showing, your love for the name of the Lord God by doing works of loving service for His people, for fellow Christians in general, or perhaps specifically for Christians in the Jerusalem congregation. You have displayed Christian love and confidence.

So, he continues, we earnestly desire that each one of you will continue to demonstrate to the end that same zeal and confidence concerning our hope in Jesus. Don't be dull and unwilling to believe; imitate the faithful and patient believers who have gone before you. (The writer will say more about this when we come to chapter 11 and also in 13:7.)

For God has given a strong encouragement to bolster our confidence and to strengthen our hope in His Word of promise (sealed with an oath He took) and in its fulfillment. Verse 19 tells us that strong comfort and the basis of our hope is Jesus. Like an anchor (but in reverse, since He is anchored in heaven above, not below us!) Jesus is in heaven waiting for us to join Him there and helping us as we make our way there. He is our forerunner, who has entered the heavenly sanctuary on our behalf, like the High Priest. He is (Psalm 110:4) the "priest forever, in the order of Melchizedek."

3 The Heart of the Matter: There Is One Way—Jesus'

So now, what has our author told us in this section of Hebrews? He has said: (1) Draw near through Jesus—that is, believe in Jesus! (2) Confess Him! Trustfully acknowledge your faith in Him. (3) Try some solid food! Don't stay on an elementary level of your knowledge of the Bible. (4) Jesus is our anchor in heaven. Holding on to Him in faith, we are secure.

Perhaps you are familiar with the finger pointing upward accompanied by the caption "One Way!" Jesus is the one way into God's presence. (4:16) "Let us then approach the throne of grace with confidence," Hebrews encourages us. For in Jesus we have the great High Priest, who has ascended into the highest heaven, into the presence of God Himself. True God and true man, sinless, He is the only human being to complete that journey—from birth, through life on earth, through death, to resurrection and ascension. But because He made it, now three things are true. The way of access to God is opened up to us; Jesus intercedes for us and presents to God His atoning sacrifice for the forgiveness of our sins; and we have an upward-reaching anchor we can hold onto with hope.

(John 14:6) "I am the way and the truth and the life," Jesus said. "No one comes to the Father except through Me." That's quite a claim. It is a conviction we find underlined in Hebrews 4–6. This claim is not popular and doesn't seem reasonable to the unbelieving world. You probably have heard that "all religions have the same goal; they are just many paths all leading to the same place." That sounds reasonable to the unbelieving world, which imagines itself to be tolerant and ready to receive truths from all directions. "Who am I, after all, to claim that the path I travel is right and another's is leading astray? Isn't it important to respect the beliefs of others? What's good and right and true for me is one thing, but for someone in another culture, something else might be good and right and true." But such seemingly humble attitudes are really expressions of doubt and unbelief. Seemingly tolerant, they are actually rejections of Jesus. They echo the cynicism of Pilate, who said, (John 18:38) "What is truth?"

No! the Word of God declares, there are not many truths, many Gods, many ways to come into the peace and blessedness of God's presence. There is one name under heaven by which we must be saved, one mediator between mankind and God, the man Jesus Christ. He is the one way.

We receive and hold on to the truth revealed to us in Jesus. We respect every person, but we do not accept the false faiths and confused notions of every person. We trust in and acknowledge Jesus, the one way. He is the trailblazer, the forerunner. He is our intercessor, our encourager. He is our anchor to our hope. He is our great High Priest.

Draw near to God with confidence through Him. Put your faith and trust in Jesus. He suffered and was obedient. He cried out to God and, after dying on the cross, was raised to life again. He completed the journey to its goal in heaven. And so He became the source of eternal salvation to all of those who hear, trust in, and obey Him.

Acknowledge Him! (Romans 10:10) "For it is with your heart that you believe and are justified, and it is with your mouth that you confess and are saved." Faith comes first, but confession is meant to follow. Baptized babies, even so young as to not speak, are believers; the gift of faith is created in them by the Word connected with the water. But they are also to be taught so that they shall both believe and confess.

To confess Jesus means to make public acknowledgment that we believe in and belong to Jesus. When Christians confess Jesus before the world, the hatred that the enemies of God showed against Jesus will also be directed against the Christians. Jesus' lot on earth is theirs too. But in heaven we also share in Jesus' lot. (Matthew 10:32) "Whoever acknowledges Me before men, I will also acknowledge him before My Father in heaven."

Try some solid food, the writer urges. Our faith and confession about Jesus are absolutely in accord with the Old Testament. This is particularly important when it comes to the conviction that Jesus is our High Priest, because the Old Testament says so much about the high priest and priests. To understand this connection involves mature spiritual insight. We must listen carefully to what the Bible tells us and make valid connections. Above all, we must accept the Word revealed in the Son, Jesus, as final and receive Jesus as the key to understanding the Old Testament correctly. Come along, Hebrews invites us. Let's read the Old Testament that way. Try some solid food!

God promised Abraham He would bless the world through Abraham's descendant, Christ. He guaranteed that promise with an oath, swearing by the only thing He can swear by—Himself. This is our doubly secured comfort and encouragement: God's promise of salvation through Jesus, a promise backed up by God's own oath. God Himself stands behind it. He says Jesus is the one way. As our forerunner, Jesus has blazed a trail straight up to heaven. As our anchor (upside down, as it were), He is fastened securely there in heaven but has left behind a rope, stretching all the way down to us to hold us and lift us up.

Conclusion

Life, as it approaches death, does get tough. Don't get stuck with an eighth grader's understanding of the faith when you run into adult-sized trials and questions. Keep learning, growing, studying the Word of God, with Jesus as the interpretative key.

Concluding Activities

Make any necessary announcements and distribute study leaflet 4.

Better and Forever

Hebrews 7

Preparing for the Session

Central Focus

Study of the Old Testament confirms that Jesus, High Priest according to the order of Melchizedek, is guarantor of a better testament, which introduces a better hope, through which we are drawing near to God.

Objectives

That participants, led by the Holy Spirit, will

1. understand that Jesus is the High Priest on whom they may rely for atonement and intercession before God;
2. be confident that God will always receive them when they come to Him through Jesus, since God has established Jesus' priesthood with an oath;
3. look to Scripture itself to interpret Scripture;
4. rely only on Jesus to bring them near to God.

Note for the small-group leaders: Lesson notes and other materials you will need begin on page 00.

For the Lecture Leader

Bible Background

The Old Testament background for this lesson is brief and, for that very reason, often puzzling. Genesis 14:18–20 leaves many historical questions unanswered. As a result, many interpreters have filled in the gaps and tried to satisfy human curiosity.

One old line of Jewish interpretation identifies Melchizedek with Shem and says "the one true priesthood" was handed down from God to Adam, to Seth, to Noah, to Shem (Melchizedek), and so to Abraham, and through him to Levi and Aaron. Another actually finds a way to turn the Bible's words upside down: Abram actually blessed Melchizedek, they say. Both of these alternatives preserve the idea of the superiority of the Levitical priesthood.

Other students of ancient history surmise that Melchizedek was chieftain (priest-king) of a local Canaanite tribe, the Jebusites. They suggest that the incident is recorded later in order to raise the status of the cult (and Levitical priesthood) in Jerusalem by showing that even the patriarch Abraham once paid homage to the priest who was "King of (Jeru)Salem."

Jewish interpreters already have an assumption that becomes the guide in their interpretation: Scripture exalts the institutions of Judaism. And the historical interpreter likewise has an assumption: the origin of the materials in the text lies in the working out of this-worldly motives, conflicts, and processes.

The author of Hebrews, who is a good model for us on the subject of how to read the Old Testament, shows none of those assumptions. He has an assumption and a process all his own. For he is a believer in Jesus, the Son of God, the full and final revelation from God. And because of that, the Holy Spirit leads him to read the Old Testament quite differently. He looks at it and asks: How does this testify to Jesus? He knows the Old Testament is the Word of God, but he will not hear it teach anything that obscures the glory of Jesus. And he will not assume that its reports are the result of human will and motives. Nor will he fill in the gaps of what the Old Testament does not say in order to satisfy curiosity or give a "reasonable reconstruction."

Indeed, his interpretation is not "reasonable" (formed by reason); it is "spiritual" (taught by the Spirit). Staying with precisely what is said (and not said) in Genesis 14, adding Psalm 110:4 and everything he knows and believes about Jesus, he comes to the conclusion that God put Melchizedek in Abram's path that day, directed their encounter, and saw to it that the composition and preservation of the scriptural report of it would be in these precise words (verbal inspiration). This was in order to liken Melchizedek to Jesus, the Son of God, and reveal beforehand, in the Old Testament itself, the superiority of the priesthood of the coming Messiah.

Our writer isn't finished working through the notion that Jesus, our great High Priest, is above and beyond the ordinary, run-of-the-mill priesthood. He's already established that Jesus' priesthood is better. He is out to underscore that even more decidedly and to impress upon us, too, that Jesus and His priesthood on our behalf is endless and eternal.

Session Plan

Worship

Begin the session with the hymn printed in the study leaflet. Accompaniments are available in denominational hymnals, such as *Lutheran Worship* (refer to hymnal index). Note: Concordia Publishing House has available *Every Voice a Song*, a 9-CD set of organ accompaniments for 180 hymns and liturgy. All the initial worship hymns in the LifeLight courses are included in this resource. It's especially helpful for mission congregations and small parishes. See the list of study resources on page 00.

Devotion

Communicating—sending and receiving messages—is a tricky business. We all know that by experience. In our everyday communicating with members of our family, the people with whom we work, and people we meet in other contexts, how often we have to say, "That isn't what I meant at all! What I meant was . . ."

Communicating requires discipline. Saying what we mean requires effort. Equally important is the discipline of listening, the other half of communicating. We have to pay attention and often check out what we are hearing with the speaker to make sure we are hearing correctly.

God communicates to us through Scripture. And listening to what God is really saying to us in Scripture also requires discipline. We have to pay attention and then check out what we are hearing by comparing it to other passages of Scripture that may be somewhat clearer. That's a basic rule of Bible interpretation: Scripture interprets Scripture. We can't interpret Scripture according to what we think Scripture ought to say or according to what we want Scripture to say.

The letter to the Hebrews requires close listening. God has something important to say to us in this week's section—something important to say about Jesus. Let's listen!

Pray together the prayer printed in the study leaflet.

Lecture Presentation

1 Introduction to Melchizedek

"What gives you the right?" we may ask when someone makes a claim on us in some way. "What gives you the right to tell me what to do?" "What gives you the right to take that?" "What gives you the right to step into this situation?"

Authority, the right to take some action, to play some role, can be important.

The author of Hebrews has just declared Jesus to be a priest—in fact, the High Priest. On what authority?

Old Testament priests were descendants of Aaron, and Jesus was not. No, but Jesus was High Priest according to a different category, or order. According to Psalm 110:4, He is a priest according to the order (likeness, category) of Melchizedek.

Who? Let's look at the only other passage from which we can learn about Melchizedek: Genesis 14:18–20.

Abram (whose name God later changed to Abraham to signify that he would become the father of many nations) was a wealthy and powerful master of a large clan. He was not permanently settled in a city but lived in Palestine as a seminomadic sojourner. In an international conflict that erupted in that area, the city-state of Sodom was one of the losers, and Abram's nephew Lot, a resident of Sodom, was taken captive. Abram pursued the abductors, rescued Lot, and brought back the goods belonging to the King of Sodom.

Genesis 14:18–20—Just as Abram met the King of Sodom to return his people and property, Scripture tells us this: "Then Melchizedek king of Salem brought out bread and wine. He was priest of God Most High, and he blessed Abram, saying, 'Blessed be Abram by God Most High, Creator of heaven and earth. And blessed be

God Most High, who delivered your enemies into your hand.' Then Abram gave him a tenth of everything."

That is all it says. There is no preparation, no follow-up. Melchizedek is a historically puzzling figure, of whom the Old Testament does not speak again until the words of Psalm 110:4, where the Lord says to the Messiah: "You are a priest forever, in the order of Melchizedek." But we are able to learn everything we need to know about the significance of Melchizedek from Hebrews 7, to which we now turn.

2 "You Are a Priest Forever": Understanding the Chain of Thought of Hebrews 7

(V. 3) Melchizedek is "like the Son of God" in that "he remains a priest forever." This does not mean that Melchizedek himself serves eternally as a priest, but that his priesthood is perpetuated by Jesus.

With the account in Genesis 14 in view, Hebrews 7:1–3 lists seven things that are stated or deduced about Melchizedek: (1) He was priest of God Most High. (2) He blessed Abram. (3) He received a tithe from Abram. (4) His name means "king of righteousness." (5) He is also "king of peace" (Salem). (6) He is without genealogy—that is, no parentage or descendants are mentioned. (7) He has neither beginning nor end, but abides, continues—because no account of his birth or death is given.

Notice that none of the requirements that would later regulate the Levitical priests applied to Melchizedek. No record is given of his parentage or of his descendants—something absolutely necessary for Levitical priests. The idea is not that Melchizedek had no father or mother, but that this information is not important in the case of Melchizedek. In his case, this information is immaterial. Scripture ignores his origin and his descendants because they have no bearing on the validity of his priesthood.

The same is true of Christ in regard to His priesthood. While it is important in one respect that Jesus' ancestry is given in the Bible to establish His descent from David as the forefather of the Messiah, His ancestry was not what qualified Him for His priesthood. Jesus' priesthood was not connected with His genealogy, just as Melchizedek's priesthood was not connected with his genealogy. Jesus' priesthood was of a different order from that of the Levitical priesthood. His was of the order of Melchizedek, where genealogy played no role.

Melchizedek remains a priest forever, since his priesthood lives on in the priesthood of Jesus, the eternal High Priest, who continues His priesthood in heaven. Melchizedek's priesthood is perpetuated in Christ. The Levitical priesthood ended with Jesus' once-for-all sacrifice of atonement, and the destruction of the temple effectively put an end to its activities. But Melchizedek's priesthood lives on in the eternal priesthood of Jesus, the Messiah, in the heavenly temple.

The Son of God, the Second Person of the Trinity, who became a man in Jesus the Messiah, was true God from all eternity. He is the original, of which Melchizedek is a shadow. Melchizedek's appearance is a prophecy that points ahead to, and reveals some things about, the priesthood of the Son of God. The historical figure Melchizedek and the way the Scriptures describe him as "like the Son of God"—that is, as a priest who foreshadows and so reveals beforehand the kind of priest the Messiah would be: one whose priesthood would be independent of genealogy, one greater than the Levitical priests, one who remains a priest forever, and one whose priesthood is established by God's own oath.

Scripture reveals that Melchizedek is a priest of a category greater than the order of the Levitical priests (7:4–10). Abram paid Melchizedek a tithe, and Melchizedek blessed Abram. Both acts show that Melchizedek's status is higher than that of Abram. Abram paid Melchizedek a tithe, even though there was no genealogical claim or law by which Melchizedek could demand it; Abram simply recognized Melchizedek's greater dignity as "priest of God Most High."

That greater dignity is also why Melchizedek blessed Abram. It is an accepted truth that (v. 7) "the lesser person is blessed by the greater." Moreover, the Levitical priests, who eventually came from the lineage of Abram, were mortal. But as Scripture does not record Melchizedek's death, his priesthood continues to live on. All of the many Levitical priests who were to be born later were present, so to speak, in the genes of Abram, when that patriarch acknowledged the greater dignity of Melchizedek and paid him a tithe.

Verses 11–19—The former law and its Levitical priesthood have now been replaced by a better one. The thesis or conclusion of this paragraph is in 7:18–19: "The former regulation is set aside because it was weak and useless (for the law made nothing perfect), and a better hope is introduced, by which we draw near to God." The assertions in that statement are argued in three separate ways.

First, when Psalm 110:4 says that the Messiah is a priest according to the order of Melchizedek, that proves the attainment of the final goal is not possible through the Levitical priesthood and through the laws that set up the Levitical priesthood and the forms of worship those priests followed and taught. For God does not duplicate His efforts. If His goal would have been attained through the Levitical priesthood, God would never have promised and spoken about another priesthood and a priest to come later.

Second, Psalm 110 speaks of the Messiah, who is the Son of David and so of the tribe of Judah (from which the Lord Jesus was, in fact, born). No member of that tribe ever approached the altar under the old Law. So, again, the prophecy of Psalm 110:4 shows that the Levitical law and priesthood had to be removed and replaced with another priesthood.

Third, the priesthood of the order of Melchizedek continues on, and the Messiah is a priest forever. His life is indestructible. The grave did not hold Him. He was raised up from the dead. All this is in contrast to the Levitical priests, who were numerous because they were mortal. They had to be replaced as they died. They had to base their claim to hold their office on regulations that depended on their ancestry, since they had to take up the unfinished work of their weak and mortal fathers, grandfathers, and ancestors. So also on the basis of an immortal life, the priesthood according to the order of Melchizedek is greater.

Verses 20–28—As the priest forever according to the order of Melchizedek, Jesus is the guarantor of a better covenant than the covenant served by the Levitical priesthood. When reading Hebrews we should remember the special nature of the covenant God makes with us. In human relationships a covenant means an agreement between two parties in which both have a part in working out the agreement—for example, the marriage covenant. But the covenant God makes is always completely one-sided. He alone establishes the terms. The other party is invited only to receive the terms.

For clarity's sake, we call that a promise. Such a promise has a guarantor, someone who puts up evidence of the good faith of the promiser—sort of a bondsman. He holds the thing promised and delivers it to those to whom it should go. Who he is and what he does and has is the pledge of the promise; it is all a believer has to trust in as he hopes to receive the content of the promise.

Jesus is that guarantor. A priest according to the order of Melchizedek, Jesus is better than the Levitical priests. The promise of which He is the guarantor is also, therefore, better than the promises they delivered as they carried out the arrangements for dispensing God's grace through the old covenant system of sacrifices.

Jesus is a better guarantor. How much better? One indication of how much better lies in the fact that God swore an oath with regard to the Messiah's priesthood. To quote Psalm 110:4 again: "The LORD has sworn and will not change His mind." No words so strong were used in connection with the Levitical priesthood. Also, Jesus is better because He remains alive to intercede for everyone, whereas the Levitical priests died and had to be replaced. Jesus is better, too, because He is sinless and has gone to heaven. He has no need to make sacrifice for His own sin (as the Levitical priests did), but He made one sacrifice for everyone and then went to heaven.

Finally, Jesus is better because He is not weak and susceptible to sin, but is God's own holy Son and has completed His atoning work and is, with an oath, installed at God's right hand as priest forever.

So we see this section begins in chapter 5 by showing things Jesus has in common with typical priests, but it concludes in chapter 7 by emphasizing those elements that are unique to Jesus as He fulfills the prophecy of a better priesthood foreshadowed by Melchizedek.

3 The Heart of the Matter

Our author warned us, didn't he? This is meaty stuff. It is an understanding of the Old Testament guided by the Holy Spirit, not by human reasoning or learning. But when we follow this line of interpretation, we begin to appreciate more and more our author's outlook and method as he encourages Jewish believers in Jesus who are hesitant about putting everything on the line for the sake of the eternal salvation promised in Jesus.

"Why should we confess Jesus and leave ourselves open to persecution?" they seem to be saying. "Don't we have reason enough to hope in salvation based on following the Old Testament? After all, isn't it the Word of God?"

"Yes, indeed it is," says our author, "and when you become skilled in the Word of righteousness, you see why it is necessary to move from the covenant with which the Levitical priests were associated to the better covenant of which Jesus is the guarantor." Because of what the Old Testament itself teaches about the Levitical priesthood and the priesthood of Jesus the Messiah, we come to the conviction that Jesus is a guarantor of a better covenant and has introduced (v. 19) "a better hope . . . through which we draw near to God."

That better hope, through which we are drawing near to God, is also important to us. While we may not feel the tug in quite the same direction as the first readers of Hebrews, or for quite the same reason, we also may be drawn away from faith in Christ. The world around us presents a full range of such tugs, from those that appeal to our intellect, to those that are plainly directed to our baser appetites. All promise a better life. Christ is better. That is still true today. Hang on to that: Christ is better.

4 Conclusion

Two issues emerge from our study this week: the priesthood of Jesus and how to read the Old Testament. Sometimes neither seems very important in the minds of Christians today. Most just don't read the Old Testament much at all, apart from a few prophecies around Christmastime. Most concentrate more on "how shall we live" than on "through whom shall we draw near"—or be drawn near—to God. Most likely very few people link Jesus' priesthood and how to read the Old Testament. Have we not heard someone say, "All roads lead to heaven," or point to the common use of the Old Testament as evidence that Jews, Christians, and Muslims all worship the same God, down deep?

It is true that Jews, Christians, and Muslims all reverence the Old Testament, but they hear far different messages, have different faiths, and worship different gods. Those who do not understand the Old Testament in the light of Christ, as is done in Hebrews 7, often arrive at false notions about the validity of non-Christian faiths.

When read as literature, the Old Testament is exquisite. When read with reason for historical information, the Old Testament may be fascinating and enlightening. When read as divine revelation testifying to Jesus the Christ, the Old Testament acquires clarity as never before.

Don't make it so hard! Don't just read the Old Testament to satisfy historical curiosity. See Christ in every page! Mature Christian students of Scripture have the Holy Spirit to help them do that. Then the claims that Jesus Christ is the one and only way to be brought to eternal bliss and communion with God will not be so hard to confess. Both things—Spirit-led and Christ-centered reading of the Old Testament, and confession of Jesus—call for us to set human reason aside and to listen to the Word of God in Scripture, in both the Old Testament and New Testament.

Concluding Activities

Make any necessary announcements and distribute study leaflet 5.

A New Covenant

Hebrews 8

Preparing for the Session

Central Focus

The priestly ministry of Christ, being better than the old covenant's priestly ministry, replaces it, even as the new covenant fulfills and takes the place of the old.

Objectives

That participants, led by the Holy Spirit, will

1. know and understand the covenant that God has established with them through Jesus;
2. trust only in Jesus as the Savior from all sin and as intercessor before God;
3. reject teachings that state that ceremonial regulations of the old covenant are still in force;
4. hear or read the Gospel daily to allow the Spirit to enter and work within their heart.

Note for the small-group leaders: Lesson notes and other materials you will need begin on page 00.

For the Lecture Leader

Bible Background

There are two key Old Testament passages behind Hebrews 8. The first is Exodus 25:40 (Hebrews 8:5). Moses, about to construct the tabernacle, is warned: "See that you make them according to the pattern shown you on the mountain." When God spoke with Moses on Mount Sinai and gave him all the instructions about the tabernacle and its worship, He showed him the "pattern" or type or model for it, namely, the heavenly tabernacle of which this earthly one was to be a counterpart, an imitation. That little word *pattern*, in the single verse Exodus 25:40, is taken as scriptural evidence to support the existence of a heavenly sanctuary.

The other key passage is Jeremiah 31:31–34, which is quoted at length (Hebrews 8:8–12). This is a passage from the Old Testament writings that spoke of the new covenant the Lord planned to make. It would surpass the old covenant He had previously made. That covenant had been broken, and the people were about to be punished by being taken into exile. But the new covenant would be characterized by the forgiveness of sins and an indwelling of the will of God in the hearts of people. If there were any doubt that the old covenant was forward pointing and to be in effect only until the new covenant should come, this passage from Jeremiah should dispel it.

Further biblical materials employed in this lesson are from the sayings of Jesus concerning His mission and the Old Testament laws: Mark 2:18–22; Matthew 5:17–18; John 5:39; and also Paul's word in Romans 10:4: "Christ is the end [the goal] of the law [the old covenant]." The point extracted from the whole scriptural testimony on the subject is this: There is only one reason why God ordered things to be as they are in the Old Testament. That is to point forward to Jesus Christ. When He came, the new covenant was inaugurated and so everything about the forward-pointing old covenant was fulfilled and made obsolete, surpassed and displaced—in a word, replaced.

There is a progression in the writer's thought, a method in his presentation. We've moved from the message to the message bearer (the apostle) to the priest. In each case the point is that, as good as the original might have been, Jesus is better. His message is certainly better (Gospel as opposed to Law); His apostleship is better (of course, since the message His apostleship brought was Gospel as opposed to Law); and His priesthood was vastly better. Now we come to really good news. The new covenant is better, much better than the old.

Session Plan

Worship

Begin the session with the hymn printed in the study

leaflet. Accompaniments are available in denominational hymnals, such as *Lutheran Worship* (refer to hymnal index). Note: Concordia Publishing House has available *Every Voice a Song,* a 9-CD set of organ accompaniments for 180 hymns and liturgy. All the initial worship hymns in the LifeLight courses are included in this resource. It's especially helpful for mission congregations and small parishes. See the list of study resources on page 00.

Devotion

To bring the Great Depression of the 1930s to an end, President Franklin D. Roosevelt executed a series of economic policies he called a "New Deal" for the American people. Of course, the basic framework of the nation's government was not changed, but some new understandings—particularly of the role the government was to play in the nation's economy—did result in some sweeping changes in the United States.

With Jesus' death on the cross and His resurrection, God established a "new deal" for all people. He established a new covenant based on grace through faith in Jesus, the Savior. This new covenant brought the forgiveness of sins and a direct, personal relationship between redeemed sinners and their gracious God.

This new covenant is the main topic of our study this week. This is the covenant we have with God. God extends this covenant to each of us individually through Holy Baptism, in which He pledges to forgive our sins for Jesus' sake and brings us into a personal relationship with Him, a relationship in which we may approach Him directly.

What a wonderful new deal this is for us! As we continue to give our attention to what the Lord is saying to us this week, may He give us hearts that respond to His new deal thankfully and with faith!

Pray together the prayer printed in the study leaflet.

Lecture Presentation

1 Introduction: Jesus on the Old Testament Law

A tradition has the bride wear "something old, something new" at her wedding. I suppose the symbolism is very appropriate, as her wedding marks an obvious transition from a previous way of life to a new way of life not only for the bride, but for the groom too.

Jesus, in referring to a wedding feast, once spoke about something old and something new and made a remarkable point. Jesus had just begun His ministry in Galilee. He healed on the Sabbath, touched a leper, cast out demons, forgave sins, and called men (including a despised tax collector!) to be His disciples.

Curious about His teachings and His relationship to John the Baptist, some people asked Jesus: (Mark 2:18–22) "'How is it that John's disciples and the disciples of the Pharisees are fasting, but yours are not?' Jesus answered, 'How can the guests of the bridegroom fast while he is with them? They cannot, so long as they have him with them. But the time will come when the bridegroom will be taken from them, and on that day they will fast. No one sews a patch of unshrunk cloth on an old garment. If he does, the new piece will pull away from the old, making the tear worse. And no one pours new wine into old wineskins. If he does, the wine will burst the skins, and both the wine and the wineskins will be ruined. No, he pours new wine into new wineskins.'"

In this picturesque way of speaking, Jesus was saying that His coming meant the beginning of a new age, one in which God's people would have a different relationship with their Lord. The period until His appearing and the beginning of His ministry, Jesus said, had been a time of waiting and a time of discipline. It was good then that people—the Pharisees, and even John the Baptist and his disciples—should have fasted.

But now, with Jesus, that for which they had been waiting had come. This is a new day, the day of the bridegroom. So let the fasting and other such forms of self-discipline cease! Let the celebration begin! This is a new day, and you cannot mix the old and the new; if you do, you will get a mess, a tear, a spill.

The Old Testament rules about touching lepers and dealing with people who were ceremonially unclean were for discipline and protection against spreading defilement in the old age. In the new age, the Messiah brings cleansing for all; He imparts wholeness to the leper and is not defiled Himself. The rules regarding working on the Sabbath were meant to point to the kingdom of God and God's rest, which Jesus would bring. When He brought it, there was no need to continue to observe these Sabbath regulations. The forgiveness of sins spoken on earth by a human voice—that was something new. But it was just that something new that the Old Testament had prophesied, even as it imposed its rules.

Now, in dismissing these Old Testament rules, Jesus was by no means showing a casual attitude toward Old Testament laws. In Matthew 5:17–18 Jesus says, "Do not think that I have come to abolish the Law or the Prophets; I have not come to abolish them but to fulfill them. I tell you the truth, until heaven and earth disappear, not the smallest letter, not the least stroke of a pen, will by any means disappear from the Law until everything is accomplished."

The Law is absolutely God's Word. Not one bit of it will fail to be true. But the laws and ordinances and institutions and events that happened in days gone by and the recording of them in the Old Testament all happened and were reported for one and only one purpose: to point ahead to the coming of Jesus. That's what Jesus said to the Pharisees in John 5:39: "You diligently study the Scriptures because you think that by them you possess eternal life. These are the Scriptures that testify about Me."

And that is also what Paul asserted in Romans 10:4: "Christ is the end of the law" (the old covenant). By no means is any of the Law left unfulfilled. All of it is fulfilled in Jesus, and so all of it is made obsolete. The new fulfills the old, surpasses it, replaces it.

2 The Old and the New: The Argument of Hebrews 8

Now we will come back to the focus of our study in this LifeLight course—the letter to the Hebrews. That point Jesus and Paul taught about Christ fulfilling the old covenant and, by doing so, making it obsolete, is the heart of the argument in Hebrews 8, the section we studied this week. This section builds on some of the thoughts in chapter 7 and, on the basis of a key Old Testament passage, makes a sweeping and bold assertion. Let's follow through the chain of thought in some detail.

Our author begins (v. 1) by summing up what he has said to this point, declaring that the ascended Jesus, seated at the right hand of God in heaven, is our High Priest. That sets the scene for what our author has to say about Jesus' service as priest and the place where it is performed.

As a priest, of course, Jesus does priestly service (v. 3). This service is performed in the heavenly tabernacle, which is the real and genuine sanctuary (v. 2). As our author has stated, God had already set up a priesthood that served in a tabernacle on this earth (v. 4). But Jesus brings the blood of His sacrifice into the heavenly sanctuary, of which the tabernacle on earth was a copy.

Verse 5—Those priests who served in the earthly sanctuary served in a copy and shadow of the true and genuine (heavenly) tabernacle. When God speaks of the "pattern shown you on the mountain" in Exodus 25:40, we become aware that there are two tabernacles. The one on earth, pitched by human hands, the tabernacle in which the Levitical priests served, is called a "copy and shadow" of the one in heaven, which is pitched by God and is characterized as genuine and real.

Verse 6—Jesus' recently begun priestly service, like the new covenant of which He is mediator and the promises on which it rests, is better than the tabernacle in which the Levitical priests served. Three times in this one short verse our author calls up comparatives: "superior," "superior," "better." He has introduced the idea of the two sanctuaries (earthly and heavenly) and the priestly service connected to them. He has previously argued the superiority of the order of Jesus' priesthood and the superiority of the laws pertaining to it. He has previously mentioned the better covenant (7:27). Now he straightforwardly asserts that the (new) covenant, the promises on which it rests, and the priestly service offered in it are all better than those of the old covenant.

Implied here and in the whole argument are two more related points, which we should not overlook. The first is in verse 6. This verse signals that something significant has happened recently. Just recently Jesus has attained this better priestly ministry. When? (8:1) When He was raised from the dead to ascend and sit at God's right hand. But until that moment—this is the other implied point—the earthly ministry of the Levitical priests in the earthly tabernacles (temple) was tremendously valuable!

Seen from the perspective of what faith sees in Jesus, the old covenant is inferior, only a "copy and shadow." But before Jesus came and had reached the goal of our redemption and revealed everything about the true and heavenly ministry, that "copy and shadow" was the best anybody had. Though a copy, it was, after all, a copy of the heavenly pattern revealed to Moses on the mountain. The earthly tabernacle, the priests, the priestly ministry they performed—all of these things were established and done according to God's command. But not for their own sake! God arranged them all that way so that they would be a forward-pointing institution and system of worship, pointing to Jesus, of whom all the Old Testament Scriptures testify, giving a shadowy revelation of the ministry Jesus would perform.

So the value of the old covenant, for its appointed time, is affirmed. Continuity between the Old Testament and the new covenant is affirmed, for the Old Testament Scriptures testify beforehand concerning Jesus. But the fulfillment in Jesus far surpasses anything in the Old Testament. And it displaces the old covenant. You cannot merge or mix the old and the new. When the new comes, it is time to leave the old behind. For in this case, the new is better.

Verses 7–13—Old Testament Scripture itself contains the better promises of the new and better covenant and its better ministry. Our author will return to the actions of priestly ministry and in what ways the priestly ministry of Jesus fulfills the shadowy pattern of the Levites, while also surpassing and replacing them (chapter 9).

For now, however, he turns to the matter of the new covenant itself and brings forward again his star witness, Old Testament Scripture. From Jeremiah 31 he quotes the promise of the new covenant. The passage includes references to the covenant established at the exodus (the "first" covenant) and then describes a "new" (second) covenant, yet to come in the future, to be established by God Himself.

The simple mention (in Old Testament Scripture, God's Word) of a new covenant, Hebrews argues, shows that God recognized the inadequacy of the people's response to the first covenant. The first covenant was not faulty—the people were. The moment God spoke of a new covenant, He made the first one obsolete. That is the author's key point here.

Let's pause to remember here that this new covenant is the covenant in which we are living. This is the covenant God has established with us through Jesus. God made this covenant with each of us individually when we were baptized or came to faith as an adult. Under the terms of this covenant, God pledges to forgive our sins and accept us as His own. We receive this covenant promise by faith, and, empowered by His forgiving love, we live as God's redeemed people in this world, giving Him our worship and service as sacrifices of praise and thanksgiving. We certainly are better off living under this better covenant! We do not want the blessings that come to us through this covenant to be lost to us through our own neglect or faithlessness. That is why we are reading and studying this letter to the Hebrews, taking to heart its warnings, admonitions, and encouragements.

Two other things deserve mention, however. First, the long quotation from Jeremiah shows the real fault with the first covenant lay in its weakness or inability to provide a remedy when the people "did not remain faithful" to it. It had no effective power to bring sinners to the heavenly goal. It only had shadowy, forward-pointing copies of a ministry that would do that eventually. But trust in those sacrifices, apart from the sacrifice of Christ yet to come, would not do any good.

However, the new covenant would be characterized by two things: the forgiveness of sins and the indwelling of the knowledge and wisdom and will of God in the heart and mind of every one of His people. This prepares for the argument coming in chapter 9, which emphasizes the effectiveness of Christ's ministry for the cleansing of consciences from sin "once for all" (9:12, 26).

A second footnote to this passage, one that is definitely a side issue, pertains to verse 13, where our author says, "And what is obsolete and aging will soon disappear." This is referring to the priestly service of the Levitical priests in the earthly tabernacle, or temple, in Jerusalem. The priestly service in that tabernacle was made obsolete when Jesus ascended to heaven. Since then it has been growing older and older.

In fact, the temple itself was then (when Hebrews was written) near to disappearing. Jesus had foretold the destruction of the temple when He spoke about it to His disciples as they were passing by the beautiful, impressive structure erected by Herod. Of that massive edifice, Jesus said, (Matthew 24:2) "Not one stone here will be left on another; every one will be thrown down."

The Jews rebelled against Rome in A.D. 66, and from 66 to 70 there was war in Palestine. But from about 68 on, it was clear that the Romans would crush the rebellion, surround Jerusalem, and most likely destroy it. And in A.D. 70, that is exactly what happened.

Could it be that our author, writing in about 68, when both he and his readers could see that Jesus' prophecy was about to come true, is referring to this coming historical event that would absolutely clinch the argument of this chapter? In general, our author is more interested in the Old Testament Scripture's descriptions of the tabernacle and priestly service than he is in the historical practices at the first-century temple in Jerusalem. But at this point he is most likely referring to the imminent demise of the historical temple and priesthood in Jerusalem.

3 The New Fulfills and Replaces the Old

This is such an important lesson: the old and the new and how the new fulfills and replaces the old. There is almost no end to the errors people fall into when they fail to remember it. Some insist that Saturday (the Sabbath) is the commanded day of worship. Some say the land of Israel should belong to the Jewish people, because that is what God promised and commanded. Some even say (in absolute contradiction to the whole message of Hebrews) that Jews do not have to become Christians to be saved, because God gave two covenants, one for the Jews (the Old Testament) and one for everybody else (the New Testament), and both are eternally valid.

Our study this week emphasizes so clearly the necessity of studying the Old Testament and New Testament Scriptures together and in the right perspective. We have a sure word of revelation in the Old Testament, but its meaning is missed unless read from the perspective of the New Testament. For there is a continuity between the two: the same God is revealing the same plan of salvation in both the Old and New Testaments. But there is also discontinuity, which comes to light as the new covenant surpasses and displaces the old. The fulfillment is more wonderful, more glorious, more surprising than anything anyone would have figured out by human logic based on the shadowy hints and promises given beforehand. And when the fulfillment comes, it means the obsolescence, the removal, the disappearance of that old setup, which was there only to point forward to the new.

You and I can read the Old Testament to find God's plan and promises to redeem us by sending a Savior. We can read the New Testament to see how that plan and those promises were fulfilled in Christ Jesus.

Something old and something new. We still have them both. But we know that, as the bride of Christ, pronounced pure and righteous because of the forgiveness of sins by grace through faith in Him, we enter into communion with God forever as a result of the real and heavenly priestly work of Jesus. He is the High Priest of the new covenant, to whom the old covenant pointed.

Concluding Activities

Make any necessary announcements and distribute study leaflet 6.

Draw Near

Hebrews 9:1–10:18

Preparing for the Session

Central Focus

Jesus' ministry fulfills and replaces the forward-pointing ministry conducted by the Levitical priests in the earthly tabernacle. To trust and believe in Him means to draw near to God by the way opened up through His ministry.

Objectives

That participants, led by the Holy Spirit, will

1. know that Christ has fulfilled the Old Testament regulations fully;
2. regard the ceremonial regulations of the Old Testament as no longer applicable in our relationship to God;
3. trust in Christ alone as the atonement for all sin;
4. draw near to God through faith in Christ.

Note for the small-group leaders: Lesson notes and other materials you will need begin on page 00.

For the Lecture Leader

Bible Background

A basic familiarity with the floor plan of the Israelite's ("earthly") tabernacle (and temple) and the regulations for the activities of the Levitical priests and of the high priest is essential if we are to understand the assertions made in this section of Hebrews. The instructions for constructing the ark of the covenant and the tabernacle are in Exodus 25–26.

Critical verses are 26:31–35, which describe the veil and the division of the tabernacle's interior space into the "Holy Place" and the "Most Holy Place." Verse 33 emphasizes that the function of the veil was to separate the Most Holy Place from the rest of the tabernacle.

Some of the daily activities of Aaron and his sons are described in Exodus 29:38–30:8: the morning and evening sacrifice of lambs at the altar and the burning of incense and trimming of the lamps inside the Holy Place. Further examples of ministrations for rites of purification are in Leviticus 14–15.

Leviticus 16 describes how only the high priest was to go into the Most Holy Place once a year with a bull whose blood would make atonement for his own sin and a goat to make atonement for the sins of the people. These actions and spaces in the earthly tabernacle have some special revelatory significance, as Hebrews 9 will make clear.

Session Plan

Worship

Begin the session with the hymn printed in the study leaflet. Accompaniments are available in denominational hymnals, such as *Lutheran Worship* (refer to hymnal index). Note: Concordia Publishing House has available *Every Voice a Song,* a 9-CD set of organ accompaniments for 180 hymns and liturgy. All the initial worship hymns in the LifeLight courses are included in this resource. It's especially helpful for mission congregations and small parishes. See the list of study resources on page 00.

Devotion

"No Admittance." "Authorized Personnel Only." We see these signs in all kinds of public places—airports, stores, and shopping malls—but churches?

There may not be such signs in churches, but are there places in church where you feel you should not go? As a child do you remember being told that you were not to go into the chancel area, especially the sanctuary (that part of the chancel where the altar stood), or that you were not to go into the sacristy, the little room in the back where altar linens and Communion ware were kept and perhaps where the pastor put on his vestments?

In the days of the Old Testament there were definitely places in the temple where ordinary worshipers were not permitted to go. There were places where only Jewish men could go. And only priests could go into the temple itself. And there was a very special place in the temple where *no one* could go—except the high priest, and he only once a year.

Usually when a place is made off-limits to the public today, it is for safety or security reasons. But the Old Testament temple was made off limits to people to make a point, to teach and remind them of the barrier between people and God. God is holy, and God's people were not holy. Unless and until they were made holy they could not come into the place where God is—and that included heaven itself.

Another point, a much happier point, was made by something else about the temple—the sacrifices made there. Some of these sacrifices made the point that God was going to make people holy with a sacrifice. The daily sacrifices that took place at the temple invited people to believe that and to know also that God was covering their sin for the sake of that coming perfect sacrifice, which would remove their sin and make them holy.

That sacrifice *has* been made in Jesus. Now we are holy through faith in Jesus. Now God has removed the barrier that stood between Him and His people. To make that clear, God Himself tore apart the curtain that set off that inner room of the temple when Jesus died on the cross. "No Admittance"? "Authorized Personnel Only"? Not any more! Now the door that leads into God's presence is open to us!

Pray together the prayer printed in the study leaflet.

Lecture Presentation

1 The New and Living Way Introduced

"Would you like to come to church with us?" Perhaps you have received such an invitation, or perhaps you've extended an invitation like that to someone else.

The author of Hebrews begins chapter 9 by inviting us to visit a worship service—the worship service that took place in the sanctuary where ancient Israel worshiped. As we stand and watch what happened there, the writer will help us understand what that old covenant worship meant. He will explain what all the thousands of bloody sacrifices offered up under the old covenant did, and he will help us see what those sacrifices did not do and could never have done.

Most important of all, he will help us see how the sacrifice our Lord Jesus made on the cross fulfilled and replaced the old covenant sacrificial system forever.

But before we go into that, let's first review what we've seen so far. The writer to the Hebrews powerfully points to Christ's superiority over the following:

* The Old Testament prophets
* The holy angels
* Moses
* The priests of the old covenant

Then, in Hebrews 8, we read that Christ has brought a new covenant, a better covenant with better promises (v. 6). This new covenant replaces the old covenant.

These have been some "meaty doctrines," tough truths for early Jewish Christians to digest. These believers struggled with making the shift from the old covenant to the new, and as they struggled, they faced persecution for their new faith. How easy it would have been for them to give up and go back to Judaism. How tempting it must have been to revert to the comfortable, familiar patterns of belief and worship. How tempting it must have been, especially in light of the fact that Judaism and those who practiced it did not draw the kind of fire that Christian belief and practice did.

But our writer urges his readers to stand firm in their Christian faith nevertheless. He reminds them that there's no going back, because there's nothing to go back to. He reminds them that the Lord Jesus has fulfilled and replaced the old covenant priesthood with all its ceremonies and regulations. Jesus Himself has become their eternal High Priest—and ours!

Now our author goes on to help his readers focus on the larger picture, to help them grasp more fully God's fulfill-and-replace scheme. In Jesus, the Messiah, God has opened up for all people a "new and living way" to approach God. The writer uses this phrase in 10:20, but the verses of chapter 9 introduce the concept.

The word *new* means "fresh" or literally, "just slaughtered." This new way to approach God involves a sacrifice, but one so different from all the old covenant sacrifices that it replaced them entirely.

This fulfill-and-replace concept permeates many chapters of the Book of Hebrews. Let's explore it further.

2 Ministries—Old and New

Imagine yourself looking at a photograph of the Grand Canyon. Imagine it's a black-and-white photo, taken from a distance.

Now imagine standing on the south rim of the Grand Canyon yourself. Imagine yourself actually experiencing the vastness, the color of the cliffs, the brilliance of the sky.

Ask yourself, what's the difference between the picture and the reality?

Now imagine attending a junior high school presentation of Shakespeare's *Julius Caesar.*

Then imagine sitting in the Roman Senate during the actual time of Julius Caesar's rule.

Ask yourself, what's the difference between the shadow and the reality?

Now imagine yourself sitting on pins and needles awaiting the arrival of a loved one who has been away from home for a long time. Imagine looking up to see your loved one's shadow falling across your front doorway.

Then imagine your loved one opening that door and falling into your arms as you hug one another in an embrace of love that seems it might go on forever.

Ask yourself, what's the difference between seeing the shadow and experiencing the embrace?

Under the old covenant, God gave His people the tabernacle to help them picture deeper realities. The tabernacle and what went on there pictured for them their Lord's own heavenly throne room and the eternal transactions that take place there.

As our writer begins chapter 9, he mentions the tabernacle and its furnishings—the lampstands, the consecrated bread, the incense, the ark of the covenant, and all the rest. Yet the things to which he refers were only shadows (10:1). They painted a broad-brush, black-and-white, from-a-distance picture of the real thing. These earthly objects and ceremonies demonstrated in a weak and incomplete way on earth the perfect and complete realities that exist only in heaven.

9:1–5—Our author refers in some detail to the layout and furnishings of the earthly tabernacle. Especially important is the veil or heavy curtain that separated the Most Holy Place from the Holy Place. The altar of incense, which stood by the veil, also probably helped maintain the separation of the two chambers, as did the smoke from the incense, which burned there daily and no doubt hung between the layers of the curtain.

If possible, refer the learners to a chart or drawing that illustrates the arrangement of the tabernacle, such as the one on page 123 of the *Concordia Self-Study Bible.*

Verses 6–10—Then the writer goes on to talk about the sacrificial system prescribed under the old covenant. He reminds his readers that the system of animal sacrifices and the old covenant priesthood was a mere shadow of the reality that was to come.

Under the old covenant, the Levitical priests represented the people to the Lord and the Lord to the people. The Lord strictly regulated their service, all of which took place at the altar or in the Holy Place.

God had stipulated that those who sinned under the old covenant were to come to the tabernacle to confess that sin. With the confession, the sinner also brought an animal, which the priest would then slaughter to pay the penalty for the sin. Day after day, month after month, year after year, the Levitical priests offered sacrifices for specific sins the people of Israel had committed. That river of shed blood—necessary to give, restore, and redeem life—was yet inadequate to redeem from sin. Isaac Watts said it well in one of his hymns:

> Not all the blood of beasts
> On Jewish altars slain
> Could give the guilty conscience peace
> Or wash away the stain.
> But Christ, the heavenly Lamb,
> Takes all our sins away;
> A sacrifice of nobler name
> And richer blood than they.

Day after day, generation after generation, the priests of

the old covenant ministered in the tabernacle's "first" or "outer" room—the Holy Place. A second, inner room was called the Most Holy Place. None of the ordinary priests ever entered it. Only the high priest could do that, and only once a year—on the Great Day of Atonement, also called Yom Kippur (Leviticus 16).

Think of it:

* The need for priests to mediate between God and His people

* The rules that made the Holy Place and the Most Holy Place off-limits for ordinary people

* The curtain that veiled the Most Holy Place and kept God's people from seeing into His throne room or glimpsing His glory

* The inaccessibility of the Most Holy Place to anyone but the high priest, and that only one day each year

All these revealed how completely sin separates sinners from the holy God. Sinners could not approach Him, dared not approach Him, on their own terms. Not because God had, in some snooty fit of rage, decided to exclude them. On the contrary, His total holiness, the white heat of His glory, would instantaneously destroy them if they entered His presence!

With that picture of holiness in mind, stop for just a moment and imagine what worship under the old covenant must have been like. Imagine yourself as an Israelite on the Day of Atonement.

Remember that on ordinary days, the priests who served you would disappear into the tabernacle to offer your sacrifices and pray for you at the altar of incense. The priests went where you could never go—into God's presence.

Now imagine the Day of Atonement. Imagine the high priest, and only he, entering the innermost part of the sanctuary. Stand outside the tabernacle in your imagination and in your mind's eye envision him walking slowly through the dimly lit Holy Place. Smell the incense and the smoke.

Picture the high priest pulling aside the heavy curtain in front of the Most Holy Place for a brief moment and then entering the darkness therein.

Imagine everyone around you standing in silence. Imagine that the only sound you hear is the faint jingle of the bells sewn to the hem of the high priest's robe. As you wait outside the tabernacle, listen for these bells as cues that the high priest has moved solemnly into the Most Holy Place and is standing near the mercy seat, the lid, so to speak, of the ark of the covenant.

Imagine the high priest sprinkling blood over that mercy seat to cover sin—your sin—so that the holy God will forego your punishment for yet another year.

What a scene! A scene that might leave even the most hardened sinner breathless with anxiety and then limp with relief.

Despite this pomp, despite the solemnity of this ritual and all the other rituals of old covenant worship, none of the repeated sacrifices of the old covenant system had any real power to deal with sin or with sin's guilt. The writer to the Hebrews makes that clear.

Verse 12—The blood of goats and calves could not bring about the forgiveness of sins or ease the pain of guilty consciences. Not even the sacrifices offered on the Day of Atonement could do that. Rather, all these sacrifices pointed ahead to another sacrifice by which atonement would finally be made, as was outlined in verses 1–10.

One day, Christ Jesus would enter heaven itself. Here, in the holiest place of all, He would spread His own blood on God's mercy seat. His blood would obtain eternal redemption. Verse 14—His blood would cleanse our consciences from acts that lead to death. His blood would atone for sin—once and for all time. In that sense, the entire sacrificial system was a kind of visual prophecy, a picture or shadow of the real thing to come.

Jesus' sacrifice of Himself on the cross fulfilled these old covenant prophecies and pictures. And it replaced them. Jesus' sacrifice differed from those of the old covenant in three important ways:

Verse 24—1. Christ entered the Most Holy Place in heaven, not the sanctuary here on earth, which was a mere shadow. He entered the very presence of the majesty of God.

Verse 26—2. Christ offered an eternal, once-for-all sacrifice, a sacrifice never to be repeated. "He has appeared once for all at the end of the ages to do away with sin."

Verse 26—3. Christ carried not the blood of bulls and goats, but His own blood. "He has appeared once for all . . . to do away with sin by the sacrifice of Himself." Hebrews 10:19—His sacrifice was enough. His sacrifice satisfied the debt we by our sins had accumulated. His sacrifice provides the basis for our confidence that our sins are forgiven and that we may approach God with a clear conscience.

Verses 16–21—This forgiveness and freedom from guilt was God's will from the beginning. It was His "testament," His covenant. The writer to the Hebrews asks us to think about this in very familiar terms—in terms of a person's last will and testament.

Verse 17—Before a person's will can go into effect, that person must die. "A will is in force only when somebody has died; it never takes effect while the one who made it is living."

Verse 22—Even the old covenant, the old testament, went into effect after a death, after blood had been shed—the blood of calves and goats. To our contemporary ears, this procedure sounds strange, even repugnant. We may think of all those bloody sacrifices and want to turn away. If so, we're not the first who have found ourselves offended by one of God's established principles: "Without the shedding of blood there is no forgiveness."

Some of our revulsion grows out of a misunderstanding of sin. How often human beings tend to think of sin as a set of infractions—mostly minor ones—or as a series of heavenly demerits in God's cosmic record-keeping system. We forget that sin is a destructive force, a power for evil that we set loose in our own lives and in the lives of those around us. Sin destroys. It came closer than we sinners want to believe to destroying God's entire creation and us, His human creatures, along with it.

Verse 23—Disastrous malignancies like this call for ghastly remedies: "It was necessary, then, for the copies of the heavenly things [the earthly tabernacle and its furnishings] to be purified with these sacrifices [the blood of animals], but the heavenly things themselves with better sacrifices than these [the bloody death of God's Son Himself]."

Or as the apostle John put it: (3:16) "For God so loved the world that He gave His one and only Son, that whoever believes in Him shall not perish but have eternal life."

Verse 28—What a comfort in life or in death. In fact, especially in death. Let the judgment come! When Christ appears in power and glory at the end of this age, He will take into His eternal kingdom all who await Him by faith.

Chapter 9 ends on a note of glorious hope. Chapter 10 picks up on the basis for that hope and expands the truths introduced in chapter 9.

10:1–2—"The law is only a shadow of the good things that are coming—not the realities themselves. For this reason it can never, by the same sacrifices repeated endlessly year after year, make perfect those who draw near to worship. If it could, would they not have stopped being offered?"

10:1–4; Colossians 2:16–17—If the sacrifices offered under the old covenant could have brought a clear conscience, if they could have effectively done away with sin, they could have ceased, their purpose accomplished. Instead, however, the annual repetition of the sacrifice on the Day of Atonement points out a consciousness of sin that would not go away.

Verses 12–13—In contrast, we have the one sacrifice of Jesus. After He had made that one sacrifice, Jesus "sat down at the right hand of God." That one sacrifice had been enough. Now He waits until His one sacrifice has made its fullest impact, the day that everyone who will receive God's gift has done so and Christ's enemies have become "His footstool." The day when sin, hell, Satan, and death are brought into eternal subjection.

Then our author introduces another scriptural quotation, from Psalm 40:6–8. Three things fall together here from this passage:

1. God's wrath against sin was not dissolved and turned into good pleasure by the many different sacrifices of the old covenant; He accepted them as a kind of IOU until they were fulfilled in Jesus.

2. God's ultimate plan was to send the Messiah (the speaker in the psalm) into this world as a true man, with a human body, to pay the penalty for sin once and for all.

3. The Messiah says: "I have come to do Your will." This refers to Jesus' life of perfect obedience and to His death on the cross, to which He went after having prayed, (Luke 22:42) "Not My will, but Yours be done." This word removes and replaces the earlier word by which God had commanded the sacrifices to be made. Jesus did God's will. Because He did, God now declares us

holy and continues to work holy thoughts, words, and actions in our lives (vv. 10, 14).

Verse 18—We can add nothing to Christ's once-for-all sacrifice; we can do nothing to earn it or deserve it. Because in Jesus there is forgiveness of sins, "there is no longer any sacrifice for sin."

This, then, makes the Levitical ministry, done in the earthly tabernacle, obsolete. Even as the writer to the Hebrews pens these words, the Levitical priesthood is about to disappear.

(V. 17) "Their sins and lawless acts I will remember no more." What a comfort we find in these words! We, of course, do remember our sins, our disobedience to God's Law. We blush with shame. But God does not remember them; He chooses to forget them. He puts them out of His mind as He draws us to His heart.

How thankful we can be for God's new covenant! How confident we can be as we look ahead, as we remember that God Himself chooses to credit the holiness of Jesus to our account.

3 Conclusion: Jesus, the New Way

What then is the way to enter the presence of God? In English, we can mean two things with such a question. (1) What is the path? (Where?) (2) What is the means or manner? (How?) Hebrews provides the answers to both questions. Jesus is both the trailblazer and the trail, the one who travels the path for us and the one who leads us along that path.

Hebrews 10:19–20 opens the next great section, one that invites us to draw near to God by faith. We'll take that up next week. But these verses also summarize wonderfully the section we studied this week:

"Therefore, brothers, since we have confidence to enter the Most Holy Place by the blood of Jesus, by a new and living way opened for us through the curtain, that is, His body, and since we have a great priest over the house of God, let us draw near . . ."

Concluding Activities

Make any necessary announcements and distribute study leaflet 7.

Now Faith Abides

Lecture Leaders Session 7

Hebrews 10:19–12:2

Preparing for the Session

Central Focus

On our pilgrimage, we should hold fast to our confession unwaveringly to the end, being strengthened to endure by a faith that looks upward to Jesus and forward to the heavenly goal.

Objectives

That participants, led by the Holy Spirit, will

1. have a clearer understanding of the nature and character of faith;
2. value the faith God has given to them by the work of the Spirit through the Gospel;
3. resolve to claim God's help in preserving, nourishing, and increasing faith in Jesus as the Savior from sin and only way to God;
4. encourage fellow Christians to stay faithful to Jesus.

Note for the small-group leaders: Lesson notes and other materials you will need begin on page 00.

For the Lecture Leader

Bible Background

Hebrews 11, one of the most beloved chapters in the Bible, speaks about faith and provides many illustrations of the power and character of faith, beginning with Genesis and continuing through incidents from the intertestamental period. It presents a host of well-attested heroes of faith from Bible times.

A reference Bible will note the key Old Testament passage behind a particular verse (e.g., Genesis 4:4 for Hebrews 11:4 or Joshua 6:20 for Hebrews 11:30). But here are four selected passages, all of them referenced in Hebrews 11, that say something special about the nature of faith.

First, reread the account of Noah in Genesis 6:5–22. The words *faith* and *believe* are not actually found in that text. But note how aptly Hebrews 11:7 summarizes what is going on.

Noah's obedience rose out of his faith. *Before* the ark-construction command, God showed him grace (*favor*, Genesis 6:8); also *before* the unseen was revealed, God declared Noah to be righteous (Genesis 6:9). God told righteous Noah of His plan (Genesis 6:13) and gave him precepts to prepare the ark. So Noah did what God commanded (Genesis 6:22). It is God who offered him grace, who declared him righteous, who gave him instructions. Noah obeys God. Noah's obedience followed his reception of God's favor. His action to build follows God's action to justify him. His obedience is a result of his acceptance of God's favor and is not the cause of God's grace. Noah's reaction to God's revelation did not cause him to be declared righteous and favored by God. Rather, by faith he received the righteousness God gave.

Second, consider Abraham and the command to sacrifice Isaac in Genesis 22. Abraham had been promised many descendants and had been told, "It is through Isaac that your offspring will be reckoned" (Genesis 21:12). In Isaac, not another subsequent substitute! For Abraham to be ready to give Isaac back to God through sacrifice and yet to believe God would fulfill His promise means that he believed God was able to raise the dead (Hebrews 11:19). When the ram was substituted for Isaac and Abraham got Isaac back, so to speak, from the dead, Abraham's faith was vindicated.

Third, Moses was led to leave his position as the son of Pharaoh's daughter and to identify himself with the Israelites and share in their ill treatment (Exodus 2:10; 5:1; Hebrews 11:24–26). This, which Moses did in faith and in obedience to the call of God, Hebrews calls "disgrace for the sake of Christ" (11:26).

Finally, the incidents referred to in verses such as Hebrews 11:35 are not all clear. The women who "received back their dead, raised to life again," could include the widows whose sons Elijah and Elisha raised (1 Kings 17:22; 2 Kings 4:35). But contrasted with them are others who suffered torture and were killed, refusing to take the easy way out. They believed in a better resurrection, into the life of the age to come, not back into this life. This could be referring to a well-known story of seven sons who were all put to death for their faith under the Seleucid persecutions of the Jews in the second century B.C. The incident is recorded in 2 Maccabees 7, and you are encouraged to read about it in the Old Testament Apocrypha. (A copy, included in some Bibles, may be located in your church library or another library.)

Session Plan

Worship

Begin the session with the hymn printed in the study leaflet. Accompaniments are available in denominational hymnals, such as *Lutheran Worship* (refer to hymnal index). Note: Concordia Publishing House has available *Every Voice a Song,* a 9-CD set of organ accompaniments for 180 hymns and liturgy. All the initial worship hymns in the LifeLight courses are included in this resource. It's especially helpful for mission congregations and small parishes. See the list of study resources on page 00.

Devotion

Do you have a hero—someone you admire greatly and would like to be like?

Heroes are common among children and young people, whose heroes are likely to be sports figures, music or entertainment personalities, or even fictional characters from movies or novels.

But adults may have heroes, too, though they may not always call them that. Someone who shows exceptional courage or leadership may be a hero.

In the section of Hebrews we are studying this week, a long list of heroes is presented to us. These are heroes of faith, men and women who displayed an exceptional faith in God in challenging circumstances. The author of Hebrews holds these faithful believers up before us and challenges us to follow their example by having faith in God in our own situations.

Our lives may not be lived in the public eye, and they may not impress others as dramatic. But our lives, too, give us opportunities to maintain faith in God through difficult times. A heroic faith is not out of our reach, for the God who upholds and strengthens His people is never out of reach but is right there beside us, ready to inspire and enable us to keep faith, a faith that glorifies God all the more as it is challenged more greatly.

Pray together the prayer printed in the study leaflet.

Lecture Presentation

1 Introduction

"Keep your eyes on the prize." Perhaps you have heard that slogan. It urges patience and persistence in a difficult struggle, because the goal is worth the effort. Don't quit shy of the goal; stick with the effort to the end.

As Christian pilgrims we are on our way to a heavenly homeland. Hebrews encourages us to persevere on that journey, to encourage one another, and not to fall away or shrink back, but to make it through all the way to the end. (10:36) "You need to persevere," it says, "so that when you have done the will of God, you will receive what He has promised."

But this journey is not easy for us. We encounter fierce temptations and tests, and we are weak human beings. Where will we find the strength to endure? An answer to that cry for help comes from a stirring Old Testament passage, Habakkuk 2:4, which is quoted or referred to repeatedly in the New Testament (Romans 1:17; Galatians 3:11; Ephesians 2:8; Hebrews 10:38–39): "The righteous will live by his faith." Through faith in God we receive strength to endure.

That principle is illustrated throughout the history of God's people in the world. In our study this week, we see what that faith is like and what it has enabled believers to accomplish. The key to endurance on our lifelong journey is to see "what we do not see" (11:1), to look up and see Jesus. The encouragement to persevere that opens this section of Hebrews leads into the long list of examples of faithful people in the Old Testament.

Let us examine the chain of thought in a little more detail.

2 Encouragement to Endure by Faith (Hebrews 10:19–12:2)

A. Four Appeals (10:19–25)

The third major section of Hebrews opens with a paragraph containing the familiar pattern of encouragement and the basis for the encouragement. In 10:19–25 the author of Hebrews sets before his readers four strong appeals. He grounds each appeal in a powerful truth.

Verse 22—First, he calls us to draw near to God with a pure heart and in full assurance of faith. This is a summary of the last section, with the idea of "faith" added. We can do this because we have Jesus as a great High Priest and, in His ministry, a new and living way to God.

Verse 23—Second, the writer encourages us to "hold unswervingly" to our confession. The idea of constancy, steadfastness, is an added emphasis. In fact, it is the main thrust of this section. We can do this because "He who promised is faithful."

Verses 24–25—Third and fourth, to pilgrims continuing their journey, our author gives encouragement to find ways to stir one another up to love and good works, and to the assembling of Christians in larger groups. We do this because of our great need for it and because the "Day," the Last Day at the end of this age, is drawing nearer and nearer.

Draw near to God in faith. Hold on steadily to your faith. Encourage one another and get together frequently. Has anything changed? Don't we still need those admonitions? Aren't these the things we continue to say to one another? When we are addressing a fellow Christian who has personal problems, don't we say something like, "Draw near to God in faith"? We may say, "Take it to the Lord in prayer" or "Let God help you." Aren't we really saying the same thing?

Or when we are speaking with a fellow Christian who is facing surgery or the death of a dear one or some other trial of faith, don't we say something like, "Hold on to your faith, and let your Lord hold on to you"? We may say it in somewhat different words, but isn't it the same thing?

Or when we are talking to a fellow Christian who seems to be slipping away from fellowship with other Christians and who is not present at worship regularly, don't we say something to that person to encourage him or her especially to gather with God's people to worship once again? These admonitions from Hebrews are as much in style now as they ever were.

And if we need the admonitions, we certainly need the reminder that Jesus, our great High Priest, has offered Himself for us. We certainly need to remember that God is faithful in keeping His promises. We certainly need to recall the Day of the Lord, that day when Jesus will come again in power and glory to bring this age to an end and to take us into His heavenly kingdom. How contemporary is this Word of God—as much in place today as when Hebrews was first read!

B. Warning against Falling Away (10:26–31)

Verse 26—Now, as he did in chapter 6, our author gives another stern warning about the danger of falling away. If a person who has received the knowledge of the truth sins deliberately, "no sacrifice for sins is left."

This does not mean that if a Christian sins, he or she cannot find forgiveness for that sin. The language here implies repeated, continuing, deliberate sin. If we persist in this kind of rebellious attitude, if we refuse to repent and to turn to God for forgiveness, our faith will eventually wither and die. We will have deliberately chosen to turn our backs on God's love and on His gracious offer of forgiveness for Jesus' sake.

God always remains faithful to His promise to forgive. But when a person who has been a Christian turns his or her back on God, rebels, and violates God's will in defiance of all of God's stern warnings and gracious invitations in Jesus, that person cannot expect to find some other way to become reconciled to God. There is no other way. There is not some other sacrifice for sin. There is only one: Jesus. In Him alone we find forgiveness.

C. Stay with Those Who Endure (10:32–39)

It is as if the writer says to the readers: "That sad end will not be true of you, will it?" In other words, he pleads: "You came through trials earlier. At times you faced persecution just because you believe in Jesus or because you stood up for and with others who were being persecuted. You faced that kind of test before, and you passed it. You've been strengthened and now have given proof, for others and yourselves, of your character. So now keep it up! Don't join those who 'shrink back' and end up in eternal destruction. Stay with those who endure and who live in heaven. Live by faith."

"Don't panic!" We often need to hear that too. If we face threats to our safety or well-being, we may feel like bailing out. At such times we need those calm, reassuring Christian friends who will remind us of the love and power of God. If we can remember times we have had similar trials before and have weathered them with the Lord's help, so much the better. "Yes, the situation is serious," our Christian friend may say, "but remember that God loves you and will keep you in His care. Remember how He preserved you in similar trials. He will preserve you again." That's what the author of Hebrews told his first readers. And that's also what the Holy Spirit is saying to us as we study this letter today.

D. Old Testament People of Faith (11:1–10)

Now our author takes us on a grand tour through the Old Testament. He mentions by name many of God's people of faith. As we think of their lives, we learn important things about faith. (See especially 11:1–3, 13–16, 39–40.)

In verse 1, the writer introduces people of faith by describing faith. It is seeing the unseen and being convinced of things not now seen. The confident faith and hope of which Hebrews speaks is far from the vague wish people often mean by the words *faith* and *hope.* ("I have faith in human nature." "I hope it doesn't rain tomorrow.") We can absolutely and completely depend upon the *object* of our Christian faith and hope—our Lord. The lives of God's faithful people illustrate that this kind of faith pleases God. In fact, verse 6 points out that no one can please God without the faith that we see exhibited so clearly in His believing people.

Verse 7—Noah provides a particularly impressive example of this. Noah *believed* what the Lord told him, even though nothing like it had ever happened before and seemed most unlikely to happen in the future. Noah *acted* on his belief; he built the ark according to God's instructions and then loaded his family on board. There they sat with all the creatures God had sent to Noah, waiting for the rain to start. As a result, Noah and the others in the ark were saved; God spared them from the disaster that overtook the rest of the world.

Name after name rings clearly from the list:

Verses 17–19—Abraham offers up Isaac in faith, believing that, if necessary, God could and would raise him from the dead.

Verses 24–26—Moses' identification with the Israelite slaves shows a faith ready to suffer abuse for the sake of the Christ.

Verse 31—Rahab's act of faith and subsequent rescue from the destruction at Jericho shows it is possible for Gentiles—even Gentile women—to be saved, a countercultural concept during that time and place, but a key part of God's plan to save the world. (See Matthew 1:5.)

Verses 32–38—This summary paragraph recounts how faith enabled God's faithful people to do great deeds and endure great suffering. What inspiring examples of heroic faith we have here!

And yet, the Old Testament also reveals these surprising facts:

* Noah disembarked from the ark, planted a vineyard, and drank wine made from his grapes until he lay drunk and naked in his tent (Genesis 9:20–23).

* Abraham lied—not once, but twice about Sarah, his wife, claiming she was his sister and thus leaving her to fend for herself in the harems of foreign rulers (Genesis 12:10–20 and 20:1–13).

* Moses committed murder (Exodus 2:11–12) and repeatedly refused God's call (Exodus 3–4).

* Rahab, before becoming a believer, made her living as a prostitute (Joshua 2:1).

On and on it goes, the cycle of human sin. How then can these people appear in what many Bible scholars have called "the honor roll of faith"? The answer is simple: God's grace in Christ. (Hebrews 10:17) "I will remember [their sins] no more," God had promised for the sake of Christ. He has chosen to wipe the record clean—just as He has done for us! Our names, too, appear on God's honor roll. He counts us among His faithful people, just as surely as He counts Abraham and Moses—all for the sake of Jesus.

All of which may cause the final comment in 11:39–40 to be surprising. This comment notes that all these Old Testament believers were stopped short of the goal. God kept them leaning forward, for He had something better in mind for them than anything they had ever known: a life in heaven forever.

But for that goal to be realized, the New Testament had to come. Only through Jesus' work did the perfection God credited to Old Testament believers actually become available. So those Old Testament believers received what God had promised them, just as we do. God did not have one set of standards and policies for His old covenant people and another set for new covenant believers.

E. Jesus, Pioneer and Perfecter of Faith (12:1–2)

Therefore, all believers, under both the old and new covenants, have one Lord who both began and finished our salvation: Jesus. Jesus leads the way to heaven and then stands at the heavenly gate to greet His followers as we arrive. We live as pilgrims on the last leg of our journey. The heroes of faith, that "great cloud of witnesses," have preceded us; they have left this world.

Still, the memory of what God did in them and through them cheers us. It encourages us to look up and see by faith what remains unseen in this world: Jesus, seated at the right hand of God the Father. Their personal histories encourage us to look ahead and see our future: the glory we will inherit with Jesus despite the abuse we may suffer on earth. He is the founder and the foundation of our faith, the trailblazer along our way. And He is the finisher of our faith, the One who will bring us through to the final goal.

3 Keep the Faith by Being Kept in the Faith

Our world is long on motivational slogans but short on knowing where to get the power needed to carry them out. The world says, "When the going gets tough, the tough get going!" But how does someone become "tough" in the first place? The world says, "Keep on keeping on." But how do we find the strength and encouragement to do that?

Perhaps you have seen cross-country runners finish a race. When the finish line comes into view, they focus every fiber of their being on it. They let it draw them, like a magnet. Through the roar of the crowd, most of the runners forget their fatigue and plant their feet one step after another up any final hills, somehow, to the finish.

But some do not make it. Oxygen-starved and disoriented, they make the turn into the last hill but lose their focus on the finish line. They fall, get up, and fall again. They will recover, but they will not finish the race.

The writer to the Hebrews urges us in our race as Christians to keep our eyes fixed on Jesus, (Hebrews 12:2) "the author and perfecter of our faith," standing at the goal. That is why participation in worship and Bible study is important. That is why Christian fellowship—talking to one another about our faith and encouraging one another in that faith—is important. Through these activities the Holy Spirit directs our eyes toward Jesus.

Our Lord Jesus did not leave us to make our way to the goal on our own. He extends His strength and power to draw us to Himself like a magnet. Because of the strength and power that come from Him, we will not be overcome by the rigors of the journey. He will always strengthen and keep us in the faith. The only way we can fall outside the field of that power is if we deliberately to refuse it. (John 10:28) "No one can snatch them out of My hand," Jesus said.

The power to help us finish this race continually flows to us from our Lord and Savior, the ascended and reigning Jesus Christ. He ran this race ahead of us. He made it to the finish line. He has blazed the trail for us. He is the pioneer of faith. Now He stands at the finish line to cheer His followers on, to strengthen and encourage us, and to give us rewards He has promised all who believe. Thus He is also the finisher, the perfecter, of our faith.

Concluding Activities

Make any necessary announcements and distribute study leaflet 8.

The Unshakable Kingdom

Hebrews 12:3–29

Preparing for the Session

Central Focus

Endure through difficulties, for you have received the unshakable kingdom; give thanks, therefore, and worship God.

Objectives

That participants, led by the Holy Spirit, will

1. recognize that the way of a Christian pilgrim is not easy but may well be lined with many hardships and suffering for Jesus' sake;
2. be willing to receive hardship and difficulty as a form of discipline sent by the Lord to strengthen and train His people;
3. regard the coming of the end of this age with confidence and joy, knowing they live in an unshakable kingdom;
4. hold on to the faith and values that are theirs in Christ, rejecting every temptation to trade in spiritual treasures for the temporary pleasures of this passing world;
5. give thanks to God for His unshakable kingdom.

Note to the small-group leaders: Leaders notes and other materials you will need begin on page 00.

For the Lecture Leader

Bible Background

Four Old Testament passages figure prominently in this section, where we continue to find the Old Testament references underlying the earnest pleas of this New Testament letter. We also continue to find a pattern familiar to us in this letter: the new continues, contrasts with, and surpasses the old.

Hebrews 12:5–11 draws several conclusions from Proverbs 3:11–12. Two points from the Proverbs passage are very important. The first is that the passage is addressed to a "son." (Following the practice of that time, the Teacher of Wisdom addresses his student as "son.")

The other point is that discipline is an essential part of teaching. The repeated references to "discipline" (vv. 6–11) and the phrase "harvest of righteousness and peace" (v. 11) might also bring to mind another Old Testament passage, Isaiah 53. There the punishment that brings us peace is laid on God's Son (the Servant). The discipline laid on God's Son restores us to wholeness. Hebrews 5:8 told us that the Son "learned obedience from what He suffered." Putting all of this together, we see that Jesus, God's Son, is our forerunner (12:3) also in receiving the discipline God lays on His children.

A section with a number of phrases from Old Testament passages, Hebrews 12:12–17 concludes with a reference to Esau. We learn from Genesis 25:33–34; 27:30–40 how, in a weary moment, Esau gave up something that would be very valuable to him in the future in exchange for a single meal, which would satisfy his present, temporary physical desires. (While Esau could not later undo the fact that Isaac gave the firstborn's blessing to Jacob, this does not mean that Esau could not be saved by faith in Jacob's descendant, Jesus.)

The description of events at Mount Sinai in Hebrews 12:18–21 is dependent on Deuteronomy 4–5 and Exodus 19. Review those chapters. Note that Hebrews emphasizes how fearful and awe-inspiring the scene was to the observers.

Finally, the concluding encouragement (Hebrews 12:25–29) rests on an image in Haggai 2:6, in which the great day of the Lord's judgment and victory is called a day when "I will once more shake the heavens and the earth." All things of this creation will then be removed. Only what God has given and which belongs to the world to come will remain: His kingdom, which shall not fall when the Day of Judgment comes.

Session Plan

Worship

Begin the session with the hymn printed in the study leaflet. Accompaniments are available in denominational hymnals, such as *Lutheran Worship* (refer to hymnal index). Note: Concordia Publishing House has available *Every Voice a Song,* a 9-CD set of organ accompaniments for 180 hymns and liturgy. All the initial worship hymns in the LifeLight courses are included in this resource. It's especially helpful for mission congregations and small parishes. See the list of study resources on page 00.

Devotion

"This hurts me more than it hurts you."

Somehow, I never quite believed that at the time—did you? Despite their assurances to the contrary, I always suspected that Mom and Dad were enjoying a little revenge when they punished me as a child.

Now that I am a parent, I see things a little differently. I see the love present when a parent must punish. But isn't it true, especially if we punish when we are angry, that we are also getting a bit even? When that does happen, it happens because parents, as well as their wayward children, have a sinful human nature.

But the Lord's motives are always pure and loving when He disciplines us, His dear children. His purpose is always to bend and send us back in the right direction. His goal is always to correct our course so that we end up where we should be. His desire is always to train and strengthen us so that, in the end, we are saved and not lost. The discipline the Lord lays on us His dear children is always a result and expression of His love for us, a love that deflected the penalty for our sins so that it ended up on His own dear Son, our Lord Jesus, and not on us. Jesus removed God's anger, leaving us the love that sometimes shows itself in the discipline God lays on His dear children.

Pray together the prayer printed in the study leaflet.

Lecture Presentation

1 Introduction

"I was told to 'Cheer up!'" goes the old joke, "'because things could be worse.' So I cheered up and, sure enough, things got worse."

The Christian life is certainly no joke, and it is not a hard-luck story, either. But the closer Christians get to the end of their pilgrimage through this life, it seems, the tougher the going gets. (Anybody living on the upper side of 45 has probably experienced that!)

There will be trouble in this world for His followers, Jesus prophesied (John 16:33). And Paul and Barnabas observed, (Acts 14:22) "We must go through many hardships to enter the kingdom of God." The path to future glory does lead through suffering.

Jesus exhibited obedience through what He suffered, and so do His followers. The people to whom Hebrews was first sent had already experienced some sufferings as Christians. And it seemed as though they might experience suffering again. And this time bloodshed might be a distinct possibility (Hebrews 12:4).

As they covered the last and perhaps the toughest miles of their pilgrimage through this life to their heavenly home, striving to endure, striving to keep the faith by being kept in the faith, how should these pilgrims regard the difficulties they would encounter? Hebrews 12 provides some answers from several angles. Let's examine the chain of thought in some detail.

2 Endure to the Unshakable Kingdom: Hebrews 12:3–29

A. Keep Looking to Jesus (12:3–4)

As you persevere through coming days of suffering, the writer counsels, keep looking in faith to Jesus and remember how He encountered opposition (12:3–4). Jesus walked the path of faithfulness and made it to the goal.

We can learn from what Jesus encountered on His journey. That faithful obedience was consistent all through the days of Jesus' humble service on this earth. But perhaps we see it most clearly at the very beginning of His ministry, when He was tempted by the devil in the wilderness, and at the very end of His ministry, in His agonized prayer in Gethsemane; in His unjust trials before Annas, Caiaphas, Pilate, and Herod; in the brutal treatment He endured at the hands of rough soldiers; in the jeers and insults of the crowd; in the rejection by His own people; and in His slow, excruciating, public death.

Take up *your* cross and follow Me, He said. The world has hated Me, and a disciple is not above His master. So you should not be surprised if the world hates you too. Christians can expect suffering before reaching the glorious goal of heaven.

The author of Hebrews has already referred to some persecutions and indignities the readers had experienced (Hebrews 10:32–34). Now he again notes that they have been struggling in opposition to the power of evil. But he says, ominously, (v. 4) "You have not yet resisted to the point of shedding your blood."

We do not know the actual circumstances of the persecution that would soon come. But, history aside, these are sobering thoughts for all Christians. Becoming a Christian, acknowledging Jesus and trusting in Him, does not mean that everything is going to get fixed in this life. The gospel of economic prosperity, the idea that faith in Jesus is the key to worldly wealth, is a hoax, quite foreign to Scripture. From Hebrews we learn differently. We learn that the path of a pilgrim, in fact, gets tougher and tougher as it nears the goal. There is obedience to be learned. There are troubles to pass through. When this happens to you, don't be surprised. Remember that the pioneer of our faith, Jesus, traveled through opposition and suffering to reach glory.

B. Do Not Lose Heart under Discipline (12:5–11)

What you are enduring is discipline. So do not lose heart if you should suffer. Recognize that this is the chastisement of the Lord, who (as the Old Testament attests) disciplines the child whom He loves (Hebrews 12:5–11). And remember too, our author says, that the Old Testament itself teaches the right way to understand these sufferings. The Lord Himself lays such chastening discipline on His son, whom He loves.

Verses 5–6—The Book of Proverbs declares that a parent-child relationship involves love and chastisement; the two are not contradictory. If they were, then we would not discipline our own children. But because we love our children, we correct their behavior, pointing out their misdeeds, encouraging them not to repeat such activity, helping them to change their attitudes and actions for the better.

Actually, love and discipline do go together, as we know from our own experience. So when we Christians experience suffering, we should not doubt that God loves us but believe all the more firmly that He does love us.

Three distinct helpful and encouraging thoughts are set forth on the basis of this idea that the Lord chastises the child whom He loves. For each one of them, the example of Jesus is illustrative. For Jesus was the Son and Servant of the Lord, on whom was laid the chastisement that makes us all whole (Isaiah 53).

Verses 7–8—First, pointing to Proverbs, Hebrews attests that chastisement is part of a father's love for his son. In fact, the son whose father never disciplines him may have grounds for grave concern. "Does this lack of caring how I behave indicate that my father does not care about me? that he doesn't love me? Does it suggest that I am not his son at all?" But as it is, the fact that God does correct my behavior proves that He does care about me and claims me as His child.

Verses 9–10—Second, the chastisement and discipline we receive from God is to be received even more willingly than the chastisement of our human fathers, for it comes from the Father "of our spirits." Our human fathers have human limitations, but God has our eternal welfare in view and is working toward that day when we will share in His holiness.

Verse 11—Third, like all chastisement, this suffering God brings upon us appears a cause for sadness in the present. But after time has gone by it gives its rewards: the peaceful fruit of righteousness to those trained with it.

A marvelous readiness to deal with reality runs through this section. Being a Christian and a pilgrim on the road to heaven does not require one to act as though this earth were already heaven. Here there is suffering. But Christians can look upon such suffering as discipline from the hand of a loving Father. In the present moment it causes sadness. But rewards will come later.

How and why these rewards come will be taken up later, but first we come to another series of statements of encouragement and warning, followed by confident assertions.

C. Keep Going; Preserve the Faith (12:12–17)

Like a coach, the writer cheers us on in Hebrews 12:12–17 as we run the race of faithfulness to Jesus throughout this life. "Keep going!" he calls. "Don't get tired now!" Don't let what this world values get in your way or trip you up. Hold on to those blessings that will last through eternity.

Verses 12–14—First comes encouragement, using language from Isaiah, Job, and Proverbs, urging us to strengthen feeble arms and weak knees and to guide our feet onto the right path, the narrow path that leads to life eternal. On this level path injured feet do not become worse, but better, with use. (12:11) God's disciplining action produces righteousness and peace. (V. 14) In that peace and holiness we are to live with one another.

Verses 15–17—Following the encouragement come three warnings. Among Christian pilgrims there should not be found any of the following: (1) Someone who misses out on the grace of God by drifting away from Christ. Living under the free gift of God's forgiveness is the hallmark of every member of this band of pilgrims. (2) A root of bitterness that springs up to cause trouble. This reference to a bitter root, from Deuteronomy 29:18, is a most enlightening illustration. From discontent comes bitterness; from bitterness comes grumbling and unbelief. Be on the watch for such a root among you, the author suggests, and nip it in the bud with forbearance and forgiveness (Colossians 3:13). (3) Anyone who is evil or worldly. To illustrate this danger, the author refers to the instance of Esau. In exchange for a helping of red lentil stew (which gave immediate but temporary satisfaction), Esau sold his birthright. The benefits of the birthright would be something Esau would not be able to enjoy until the future, but they were far greater and longer lasting.

Esau is a great example of someone who squanders away future wealth for immediate satisfaction. Our author does not want us to exchange our future in heaven for the temporary advantage of safety and freedom from pain in this life.

That temptation comes to us also. Jesus warns that someone who gains even the whole world but loses his or her soul in the process has made a poor bargain. By the way, when Hebrews says that Esau could not later change his mind, it means he could not get back the firstborn's blessing Isaac had given to Jacob. It does not mean Esau could not repent of his sin and trust in Jacob's descendant, Jesus, for the forgiveness of all his sins.

D. Christians Have Come to the Better Mountain (12:18–24)

Following the encouragement and these three warnings comes another positive statement that expresses confidence about the readers (see 6:9; 10:39). This statement contrasts two mountains: Sinai and Zion. It emphasizes again that those who believe in Jesus must now see themselves as distinct from Judaism. Certainly there is continuity from the Old Testament to the New Testament. And certainly Christians continue to use the Old Testament, but here the emphasis is on how the new covenant fulfills and replaces the old covenant. The new covenant contrasts with and surpasses the old covenant.

Think what it must have been like to have been present at Mount Sinai when God revealed His Law! Think about the fire, the darkness, the storm, the loud sound of trumpets that came from the top of Sinai! The mountain was holy and could not be approached. Even Moses himself was afraid. But Judaism, which exalts that event as the most important ever, Hebrews says, is a religion that stays in this world. For that mountain, Sinai, "can be touched." It is material, a part of this world, and can be seen with human eyes and felt by human hands and feet. Everything associated with the giving of the old covenant based on the Law was material and physical.

But when we come to the new covenant God has made with us in Christ, we have come to a different mountain, one where only the spiritual eye of faith can see its reality, its truth. This mountain is Mount Zion—that is, the heavenly Jerusalem—and everything associated with it can only be seen by faith. It is different from, better than, the fulfillment of, and replacement for that touchable mountain, which is limited to this world.

What a contrast! The heavenly mountain, Mount Zion, towers over the earthly mountain, Mount Sinai. The new covenant surpasses and replaces the old covenant.

It is to that heavenly mountain, that new covenant, that we have come. Why go back?

E. Appeal and Comfort to Recipients of the Unshakable Kingdom (12:25–29)

With what a remarkable comfort and what an appeal the author concludes this section! We are the possessors of so many heavenly realities. We who believe in Christ have the pearl of great price, the possession that will never lose its value. But watch out, Hebrews tells us. The penalty for ignoring God when He spoke from Sinai, that earthly mountain, regarding a temporary covenant could not be escaped. How much greater will be the consequences if we ignore God when He speaks to us from the heavenly mountain regarding an eternal covenant!

Verse 26—The earth shook back then at Sinai; God's voice shook it. But that same God has announced that one day He will "shake not only the earth but also the heavens" (v. 26, quoting Haggai 2:6). This shaking will be the final shaking, because it says "once more." Verse 27—Then, not just an area around Sinai, but everything that can be shaken, everything "created" (belonging to this creation), will be removed. Only things that cannot be shaken, things that do not belong to this world but to the world to come, will survive that shaking. Those surviving things are what God has now made anew, the new creation in Christ. The children born of God in Christ, the rule of God among people in Christ, the angels, those who have been made holy through faith in Christ—these belong to the unshakable kingdom.

Verse 28—That kingdom God gives as a free gift in His Son, Jesus. Believers in Jesus have received the unshakable kingdom. This is comfort. We are encouraged not to forfeit it by giving it up for some this-worldly value. And we are encouraged to show thanks to God and to worship and serve God with reverence and awe. This is the appeal. Verse 29—"For our 'God is a consuming fire.'" He is a supernatural kind of fire, such as was revealed at the burning bush, which burns in and of itself and does not destroy what is holy, only what is unholy. This fire is not a natural fire, the fire of this world, for God is a power from beyond this world. The fire consumes sin and purifies God's people by burning away the ungodly aspects of their lives. Here are warning, comfort, and appeal.

What a treasure God has given us in the Gospel of Christ! It is a treasure that, while often unappreciated in this world, causes all of the treasure of this world to be insignificant by comparison. And yet, how many pass by the heavenly treasure and eagerly fight over the cheap and crumbling treasures that seem to glint and gleam in this world.

Christians, don't be taken in by this eager grasping around you! See that the treasure God has placed in your hands is infinitely more precious and long lasting! Don't trade it away for the worthless goods of this world, which offer only a momentary pleasure that soon turns to bitterness. You have a kingdom that lasts, that is unshakable. Hold on to that unshakable kingdom!

Concluding Activities

Make any necessary announcements and distribute study leaflet 9.

Pilgrims' Worship

Hebrews 13

Preparing for the Session

Central Focus

Concluding his sermon-by-mail with various appeals, greetings, and blessings, the author gives concrete advice to pilgrims about their life of worship in thanksgiving to God.

Objectives

That participants, led by the Holy Spirit, will

1. understand and accept the exhortations addressed them in this closing chapter of Hebrews;
2. desire to worship God with heart, lips, and life;
3. desire to be cooperative and obedient to spiritual leaders who speak the Word of God;
4. trust in the Lord Jesus Christ as the eternal and all-sufficient Savior.

Note for the small-group leaders: Leaders notes and other materials you will need begin on page 00.

For the Lecture Leader

Bible Background

Even in this concluding chapter, where argument tends to yield more space to encouragement, the reliance on the Old Testament background is evident. One finds one quotation (Psalm 118:6–7 is quoted in Hebrews 13:6) and numerous allusions (to Deuteronomy 31:6 in 13:5; to Hosea 14:2 in 13:15; and to Ezekiel 37:26 in 13:20, to name a few).

But there is also one challenging passage that seems somewhat dark until one studies carefully the biblical background for it in the Old Testament. Hebrews 13:10–13 depends on several details in Leviticus 16. When the goat and bull were sacrificed on the Day of Atonement, the high priest brought the blood into the Most Holy Place. But, unlike the practice in the case of other sacrifices, the bodies of that bull and goat were taken outside the camp to be burned. Great sin and iniquity had been transferred onto them, and so their disgrace was borne outside the camp. The priests and worshipers did not eat the meat of these sacrifices. It is important to review Leviticus 16 once again for the study of Hebrews 13:10–13.

Session Plan

Worship

Begin the session with the hymn printed in the study leaflet. Accompaniments are available in denominational hymnals, such as *Lutheran Worship* (refer to hymnal index). Note: Concordia Publishing House has available *Every Voice a Song*, a 9-CD set of organ accompaniments for 180 hymns and liturgy. All the initial worship hymns in the LifeLight courses are included in this resource. It's especially helpful for mission congregations and small parishes. See the list of study resources on page 00.

Devotion

Perhaps when you saw the title of this week's study leaflet you thought it might be about church services. That's probably what crosses our minds first when we hear the word *worship*.

Of course, worship in church is highly important, and the writer of this letter has had quite a bit to say about God's people getting together for worship. He has referred extensively to the worship that took place in and about the temple under the old covenant. He has urged believers under the new covenant to get together frequently and regularly for services of worship.

But this chapter is not about formal worship services. This chapter refers to the continuing worship that we Christians give to God as we go about living our faith every day. In verse 15 of this last chapter of Hebrews, the writer urges us to "continually offer to God a sacrifice of praise—the fruit of lips that confess His name." And then he immediately adds, (v. 16) "And do not forget to do good and to share with others, for with such sacrifices God is pleased."

This letter has had a lot to say about sacrifices, especially in contrasting the sacrifices of the old covenant with the once-for-all sacrifice Jesus made for our atonement. But now it refers to another type of sacrifice, the sacrifices we Christians offer to God in thanksgiving and praise to the Lord. These are sacrifices we can and do make each and every day, as we go about with praise for Jesus on our lips and in our hands (as we serve others for His sake). These are sacrifices, offerings to God, that please Him, because they come from hearts that look to Him with faith.

Pray together the prayer printed in the study leaflet.

Lecture Presentation

1 Introduction

Worship. That's something that happens in church. Right?

Not necessarily! We know that worship happens more often and in more places than that. We worship God whenever we praise Him and let Him know how much He means to us. And you don't have to be in church to do that. Sometimes you don't even have to use words to do that, though it would be hard to imagine real worship going on very long without using words. In this last chapter of the Letter to the Hebrews the author encourages us to give God our worship continually.

Perhaps you remember how the author ended the previous chapter. Assuring his readers that they have received an unshakable kingdom, the author comforts and encourages them in Hebrews 12:28 by saying, "Let us be thankful, and so worship God acceptably with reverence and awe."

In this concluding chapter, our author continues that encouragement with some direct advice and words of blessing. (V. 16) "Do not forget to do good and to share with others, for with such sacrifices God is pleased."

Doing good and sharing with others—those are the two broad categories in which the various commands we find in chapter 13 fall. Doing all such things is worship, the kind of things pilgrims do, out of reverence and awe of their God. Let's look a bit more closely at the specific instructions and commands we find in this last chapter.

2 Pilgrims' Worship (Hebrews 13)

Hebrews, it has been said, begins like a sermon and ends like a letter. Hebrews does not begin in a customary way for a letter; the author does not name either himself or his addressees, as Paul does, for example, in Galatians. But this last chapter of Hebrews is very much like nearly all of the other New Testament letters. It contains miscellaneous instructions and information (vv. 1–19), a formal benediction (vv. 20–21), personal notes and greetings (vv. 22–24), and a brief concluding blessing (v. 25). Most likely the public reading of this letter was meant to conclude at verse 21.

A. Seven Simple Commands (13:1–7)

In the opening seven verses of Hebrews 13 we find seven straightforward commands, words that tell pilgrims how to behave in a way that will give thanks and worship to God. Along with the commands there is—as we have come to expect in Hebrews—an Old Testament passage that provides support.

Verse 1—"Keep on loving each other as brothers." Verse 2—"Do not forget to entertain strangers." The first command is one we might expect. Of course we will love and care for our "brothers," for they are our kin. That should continue. But then there are the strangers—travelers, people from someplace else. The writer encourages showing hospitality also to them. A band of pilgrims on the road may include persons from many families and groups. Hebrews urges welcoming one another, just as Paul had earlier encouraged the several groups in Rome: (Romans 15:7) "Accept one another, then, just as Christ accepted you, in order to bring praise to God."

Notice the reminder that, in welcoming strangers, some had unknowingly entertained angels. In our study this week we read how that had happened, and we also read how Jesus tells us that when we welcome a fellow Christian in His name, He counts it as if we had shown Him our hospitality.

Verse 3—"Remember those in prison . . . and those

who are mistreated," as though you are right there with them; in fact, you are. As members of Christ's body, we share troubles as well as triumphs. Verse 4—"Marriage should be honored by all, and the marriage bed kept pure." Pilgrims on their journey honor their Creator and respect the bodies He created by keeping their sexual behavior within the boundaries God established for these appetites.

Verse 5—"Keep your lives free from the love of money." We can be content with what we have and even rejoice in it, because we know what Paul called "the secret" of facing plenty or want (Philippians 4:12–13). The Lord, who will never forsake us, is our strength and help. The Lord looks after His own. Trusting this truth, the child of God is content with what the Lord gives. The energy and time spent on worrying and stockpiling money is better devoted to the work of God's kingdom.

Verse 7—"Remember your leaders," the writer says in a tone suggesting that some of these leaders may have passed out of the pilgrim band and into the cloud of witnesses (12:1). "Consider the outcome of their way of life and imitate their faith." Here the theme we found in chapter 11—taking encouragement from the heroes of faith who lived before us—is sounded one more time.

Now the writer holds up as examples for their faith their own past leaders, people they had known personally. Remember how the faith of your leaders sustained them and kept them steady to the very end of their lives on this earth. Their departure from this life and the result of their way of life are worth thinking about. We can learn from what they show us about faith and about steadily trusting the Lord to the end. Right here in verse 7 we are given a reason for keeping alive the memory of faithful Christians from our own time and for studying the lives—and deaths—of heroic saints and martyrs from the past ages of the Christian church.

B. A Word about Jesus (13:8)

Concluding this string of seven commands regarding behavior and linking the string to an eighth command is a remarkable verse. Hebrews 13:8 is often misunderstood. Many have explained the verse as an isolated statement about the eternal unchangeableness of Jesus Christ, true God: "Jesus Christ is the same yesterday and today and forever."

It is true that Jesus Christ is true God and, as God, is unchangeable. But let's relate this statement more closely to its context. "Yesterday" does not necessarily mean "from eternity," and the actual word order suggests this translation: "Jesus Christ yesterday and today is the same and also forever." It says that the God-man, Jesus Christ, who recently (yesterday) lived and died, learned obedience through what He suffered, was brought to the goal of accomplishing our salvation, and entered heaven to sit at God's right hand and intercede for us. He continues as the same Savior today—and forever.

This declaration about Jesus is the basic truth that stands behind and supports the encouragements regarding daily life that have just been stated. Jesus Christ, crucified and exalted, to whom their leaders looked in days gone by, and by whom these leaders were kept steadfast in the faith to the end of their lives—that Jesus is still there for us today. We can look up to Him today and be strengthened for our own journey of faith.

Jesus, in His unique position as the One who brought about our salvation, rules in heavenly power to guarantee our salvation forever. He lives and rules eternally—until the devil and all his powers and all those in this world who serve the devil's purposes are completely under Jesus' control. What encouragement this is for us as we struggle to live as God's people in this world! Our Savior rules from heaven, and He is as intent on our salvation now as when He died on the cross and rose again from the grave.

C. Pilgrims' Unique Fellowship (Hebrews 13:9–16)

Verse 9—Now the author warns his readers not to be carried away by the many different kinds of teachings surrounding them that do not come from God. Throughout the New Testament world Christians seem to have been confronted with superstitious notions concerning regulations about food. Christian leaders had to insist over and over again that grace, not food, gives us a sound basis for confidence before God. Salvation is by grace alone. Nothing else—neither anything within a person nor anything outside a person—can be relied on to forgive sin, cleanse the conscience, and purify the heart.

Verses 10–13—Then comes a passage that underlines once again the separation of the Christian faith from

Judaism and any other religion that emphasizes rules and rewards that only affect life in this world. To make this point, the author refers to the Day of Atonement under the old covenant. Usually the old covenant priests were permitted to eat a portion of the sacrifices they offered. But not on the Day of Atonement! On that day not any portion of the bull or the goat that was sacrificed could be eaten by the priest or by anyone else. For the sins of the priest were laid upon the bull, and the sins of Israel were laid upon the goat, and both animals became unclean. Some of the blood of the goat and bull sacrificed on the Day of Atonement was taken into the Most Holy Place, but the carcasses of the animals were taken outside the camp and burned. Much sin had been transferred to those bodies, and they had much disgrace and reproach upon them. So they had to be destroyed outside the camp, not consumed by the persons who worshiped or served at the tabernacle. (Exodus 29:14; Leviticus 6:30; and other texts retell how the sin-laden inferior animal sacrifices were burned outside the camp, a picture of a sin-laden and guilt-bearing Christ, who is literally crucified *outside* Jerusalem's city walls.)

The "altar" at which Christians worship is the one foreshadowed by the Day of Atonement ritual: the throne of God in the Most Holy Place in heaven. The sacrifice whose blood purifies us is that of Jesus Christ, foreshadowed in the Old Testament by the bull and goat on the Day of Atonement. Just as with the bull and goat, His body was destroyed "outside the camp," for He suffered crucifixion, bearing shame and reproach, on Calvary, outside the walls of the city of Jerusalem. So Leviticus 16 teaches us again to expect a different and better kind of altar, sacrifice, and worship from what was cherished by the old covenant. For that ritual could only cleanse the physical bodies of worshipers, while Christ's sacrifice cleanses the soul before God in heaven.

Verse 15—This all fits together with the fact that the kingdom to which we belong is not of this world. Rather, it is of the world to come. Our citizenship is in heaven. Therefore, our worship is not wrapped up in physical things, with physical animal sacrifices, or with eating (or refraining from eating) certain foods. Our worship is a "sacrifice of praise—the fruit of lips that confess His name."

This includes the behavior described in the seven commands of verses 1–7, and it includes the unique fellowship of the Christian pilgrim band suggested by verse 13: "Let us, then, go to Him outside the camp, bearing the disgrace He bore." To Jewish Christians—afraid to break with Judaism and be known simply as Christians and face persecution—this was a powerful, meaningful admonition. To all of us who cling to the comforts and values of this world and are not inclined to cherish heavenly and eternal blessings when this involves suffering, here is a call to leave behind the comforts of camp and get out on the road with the pilgrims! That road includes a God-pleasing life and sharing in Jesus' humiliation and suffering. This is the worship that pleases God.

D. Further Pleas (13:17–19)

Verses 17–18—Two further requests are made of the readers. Both of them seem particularly appropriate for us as well: "Obey your leaders and submit to their authority" and "Pray for us." The writer explains more fully what he means. Here we have a formula for a happier church or Christian fellowship. God entrusts to Christian leaders the responsibility for watching over the souls of those in their congregations. They must account to God for those souls. If any one is lost, these spiritual leaders will be held accountable. So they are very careful and concerned. When their followers obey willingly, leaders may more easily serve with joy instead of grumbling, and that is all the better for the followers too!

We know this to be true from our own experience. When congregations cooperate with their pastors, everyone is happier—congregation and pastors too. But when pastors have to deal with constant resistance from the congregations they serve, when pastors must beg and cajole and even threaten to receive the cooperation they need to do their work, everyone is discouraged. (The same holds true, of course, for cooperative congregations who suffer with a recalcitrant, uncooperative pastor.)

The author also requests the prayers of his readers. He has been sincere with them. His conscience is clear; his only desire has been to behave nobly toward them. Verse 19—Above all, he wishes to see them soon again in person, and he expresses that desire. He asks that his readers join him in this prayer. We remember that our spiritual leaders also desire that we support them in our prayers. Our prayers will bring blessings upon their ministries and guard them from the attacks of the devil and the opposition of the unbelieving world.

E. Formal Benediction (13:20–21)

Verse 20—The author's benediction in Hebrews 13:20 is one of the great treasures of the Bible. God is "the God of peace." He brought our Lord Jesus up again out of the dead. Jesus is characterized as "that Great Shepherd of the sheep," which He is "through the blood of the eternal covenant."

Verse 21—God is called upon to equip the readers—and us—with all manner of good things so that they (we) can do God's will, that which "is pleasing to Him, through Jesus Christ." Unless the work be done in faith and presented to God through Jesus, it is never pleasing to God.

The blessing ends by giving all glory to God. As members of the congregation pray for their pastors, pastors pronounce a blessing upon the people they serve, asking God to make them able, ready, and willing to do those things He desires from us in our daily activities and contacts.

The chief themes of Hebrews reappear here: the eternal covenant, the work of God in Jesus, the faith of God's people, and their worship through Jesus. It is a capstone to this lofty letter, which ties the entire Bible together so magnificently.

F. Personal Notes; Brief Blessing (13:22–25)

The public reading of this letter probably concluded with the Amen after 13:21. The remaining verses are a few words of personal communication to a group of leaders or friends among the addressees.

Verse 22—The author makes a plea that his letter be received with patience, making the humble comment: "I have written you only a short letter." We marvel at that remark, considering the length and depth of Hebrews and the care of its construction! He here identifies his work as a "word of exhortation," a term often used to refer to a sort of sermon or address in a service of corporate worship.

Verse 23—He includes a note of news: Timothy has been released. This is news to us, too, who have no other knowledge than this that Timothy had been taken captive! It is a fascinating hint about the life and trials of church leaders in the last half of the first century.

The fact that there is no mention of Paul suggests that this letter was written after his death, probably in the mid 60s. (While some have suggested that Paul himself wrote the letter, most professional Bible scholars dismiss this suggestion on the basis of the great difference in writing style from the letters identified as coming from Paul.)

Verse 24—Greetings are sent to all the leaders and all of God's people (Christians). Greetings are included from "those from Italy." It is not clear whether that means persons originally from Italy and now living elsewhere are sending greetings back home, or whether it means that persons native to Italy are sending, from Italy, greetings to the readers. Verse 25—The simple closing blessing sends to the readers what every Christian most needs: "Grace [God's favor] be with you all."

3 Conclusion

So we come to the end of a remarkable word of encouragement. It really is not such a difficult book, and its message is, in fact, quite clear and plain. Listen to Jesus, the Son. Draw near to God with confidence through Jesus, the High Priest. Endure to the heavenly home by looking up to Jesus, the pioneer and finisher of faith. Don't conform to this world. Join the pilgrim band on the road that leads to glory. Heaven is our home!

Concluding Activities

End with a brief prayer thanking God for the blessings received through this study of His Word.

Make any announcements (including information about the next LifeLight course). If your schedule so suggests, distribute the first study sheet of the next LifeLight course.

Small-Group Leaders Material

Listen to the Son

Hebrews 1–2

Preparing for the Session

Central Focus

We are like pilgrims who need a word of encouragement; Hebrews encourages us to listen to the Word of God revealed in the Son of God, Jesus.

Objectives

That participants, led by the Holy Spirit, will

1. recognize that Jesus is the decisive revelation of God to us;
2. be aware of angels as the servants of God for our sake;
3. be confident that Jesus has overcome the power of the devil, sin, and death by His perfect completion of all that is required for our salvation;
4. honor and worship Jesus as the Son of God.

For the Small-Group Leader

If this is your first go at facilitating a LifeLight small group, you're in for a happy and exciting experience. It isn't essential that you have special expertise. What you need and want is good rapport with your group. That's just a matter of liking people, wanting to help them, and now and then being assertive enough, without being stuffy, to act as your group's friendly, neighborhood traffic cop.

You're the one to get things started when it's time to start. And you must stop things when it's time to stop. (That's not always easy when the discussion is in full swing.) And you are the one to direct traffic down the right streets and around the right turns to get to the point of the discussion. But mostly you are there to listen, to make sure everyone gets a fair chance and that no one feels any the worse for having been a participant in your group activity. No one expects you to be a master teacher. You are one of the group, albeit the one with "the book," which gives you just that edge needed to be the leader.

Here are things you may want to keep in mind to help you be the facilitator, the leader.

1. These three questions will help your group study the Bible: What do the words say? What do the words mean? What do the words mean to me? Much small-group discussion can be lubricated by resurrecting these three questions now and again.

2. Scripture interprets Scripture; we don't. Some Bible "scholars" interpret the more difficult and obscure passages of the Bible on the basis of their own knowledge, wisdom, or best guess—or, even worse, on what they fervently wish would be so. God is the author of Scripture. He does not contradict Himself. Any understanding of Scripture not in agreement with other, clear passages of that same Scripture is simply wrong. To understand the words of Scripture it is necessary, proper, and scholarly to compare them with other words, other parts, indeed, all of Scripture. For this reason much of the self-study your group will do in the next nine weeks will call for cross-referencing passages from many parts of the Bible. Note: Questions sometimes quote passages; quotations are from the New International Version (NIV) unless we indicate differently.

3. Being right is not, in itself, the magic goal. Don't misunderstand; error is to be avoided and corrected. But when the members of your group are asked each week to share the results of their study, the purpose is to encourage one another to read, study, and share God's Word. When someone wanders from the point or is blatantly in error, help the group, through its discussion, gently to help the person see what Scripture is really saying. So you as leader might from the outset avoid responses such as, "No, you are wrong" and substitute instead, "That's interesting. Does anyone have any ideas about that?" or "Yes, but the writer of the questions has a different slant on that. The answer he provides says this. What do you think of that?"

It may be helpful to mention that the author of Hebrews had no intention of arranging it into nine convenient sections with five more or less equal parts in each to accommodate the structure of the LifeLight Bible Study Series. As a consequence, our divisions may seem contrived at times, but they seek to accommodate the author's message.

What follows are some comments about the daily assignments in the student study leaflet. It is assumed the student has worked through the questions and is prepared to share his or her work with the other members of the group. The questions are arranged so that one-half hour of study invested each weekday will be enough to finish the week's assignment.

Small-Group Discussion Helps

Day 1 • Hebrews 1:1–3

Remind the participants to read the assigned portion each day. Refer participants to the three questions mentioned earlier: What do the words say? What do the words mean? What do the words mean to me?

1. The Bible records many different ways in which God communicated with people. The passages cited refer to five of them: through dreams (Genesis 28:10–13), miraculous signs (Exodus 3:1–4), audible voice and writing on stone tablets (Deuteronomy 4:12–13), and prophets (2 Chronicles 24:19). Perhaps participants will be able to recall other biblical examples of ways in which God communicated with people.

2. "We know a little bit about a lot of things." But if God had not set out to instruct us, there are some things no amount of thought or study or discovery would have revealed. Three of these referred to in the passages listed are (a) Jesus is God; (b) God created the universe through Jesus; and (c) salvation is by grace.

3. The writer of the epistle makes the point in 1:1–2 that there was a message from God in the Old Testament. Now there is another. Stage 1 is the message delivered by the prophets. Stage 2 is the message delivered by Christ.

4. The Son accomplishes in His incarnation, suffering, and death what the high priest pictured and signified in his yearly sacrifice of an animal on the Day of Atonement (Leviticus 16:30). Once for all, on Calvary, the Son atones for the sins of the world. He did this out of love (Ephesians 5:25), in order to make the church, His bride, holy and perfect. All this He did, not because of our goodness, but because of His mercy, even working in us through His Spirit and Baptism the faith by which we accept His forgiving love (Titus 3:5–7; 1 Peter 3:21).

5. Psalm 110:1 pictures the coming Messiah as a king with defeated enemies at his feet. (As in Joshua 10:24, victorious kings placed their feet on the necks of their prostrate, defeated enemies.) The Ephesians text teaches that Christ, as true man, is not only present everywhere, but also now fully exercises this divine power over the whole universe for the benefit of His kingdom and the upbuilding of His church. (Note: This belief, often repeated as we confess our faith in the words of the Apostles' Creed, should not lead us to picture Christ as far away and inactive but, on the contrary, as our active-for-us Prophet, Priest, and King.)

6. "In these last days" indicates that the last and final revelation has already come in Christ. Thus we have absolutely all we need or shall receive to achieve the gift of life. In the light of that promise we must be wary of the false claims of latter-day prophets and non-Christian religions that claim revelations after the New Testament (e.g., the Mormons, Muslims, TV evangelists, and others who claim they've received new and direct revelations). Instead of being caught up in every new wind of doctrine or purported additional revelation, we need to go ever deeper in our grasp of Holy Scripture. All we need and everything we ought to cherish is ours and fully revealed in God's Word.

Day 2 • Hebrews 1:4–14

7. (a) Jesus is God's Son. (b) The angels worship Him. (c) While the angels are as speedy as winds and as powerful as fire, the Son is God (v. 8). According to His human nature, Jesus has been elevated by the Father as King over all the saints (Revelation 3:21). (d) Jesus created the heavens and the earth and is eternal. (e) Jesus reigns with God the Father on the heavenly throne; angels are sent by God to help and serve God's people.

8. God promises that He will send His angels to watch over and protect us, even from physical harm. The angels are agents of God in caring for us. While we are not to tempt the Lord by putting ourselves deliberately in harm's way, we can have confidence in knowing that the Lord sends His powerful, invisible army to watch over us.

Day 3 • Hebrews 2:1–9

9. The "therefore" refers to "what we have heard"—that is, what chapter 1 has outlined—the message of all the Scriptures as it focuses on the Son of God, who "provided purification for sins" (1:3). Christ is so much "superior" to the angels and He is so far above any and all, that His message calls for serious attention.

10. The angels are said to have delivered the message of the Law, as distinct from the Gospel.

11. Christ's Gospel is mankind's only hope. Apart from Christ, there is no salvation.

12. Angels will not rule over heaven. There they will join the saints in praising and worshiping God. Probably they will also continue to serve God and His church there, even as they do now.

13. Our sin deserves and leads to death—eternal death and separation from God. Only God could atone (pay) for the sins of all people. Only a human being could die. Thus the Son of God became incarnate (human) to keep the Law for us and to die in our place. Jesus tasted death for all people. He is our substitute.

Day 4 • Hebrews 2:10–15

The idea of Jesus as our substitute continues.

14. "Perfect" means "complete." Jesus fully and *completely* accomplished our salvation through His innocent suffering and death; nothing more needs to be done. Peter tells us that He "died for sins once for all, the righteous for the unrighteous, to bring you to God" (1 Peter 3:18).

15. Jesus is "of the same family," "like His brothers in every way" (v. 17)—except that Jesus remained pure from sin. Because Jesus was our brother and one of us, that is, a true human being, He qualifies as our substitute.

16. By dying and rising again for us, Jesus took the "sting" and fear out of death. As Jesus died and rose, so we, with Jesus, will survive death and with glorified bodies enter everlasting life with Him in glory.

Day 5 • Hebrews 2:16–18

17. Abraham's descendants are all those who share His faith in the redemption that God would bring about through the Savior. Abraham anticipated the Savior who would come; we believe in the Savior who has come. That is the main difference. Abraham's spiritual descendants include both Jews and Gentiles.

18. The example sets the pattern for considering the two additional temptations. Matthew 4:5–6: the temptation was to jump from the temple into the midst of those below. The implication was to win the people by a spectacular demonstration of power as opposed to the way of the cross. Time permitting, a profitable discussion could revolve around our desire sometimes that God would win the world to our faith by some powerful demonstration of the validity of our convictions. Matthew 4:8–9: the temptation was to worship the devil. The implication was to acknowledge Jesus' need for Satan's power to accomplish His ends.

19. In each instance, Jesus overcame the temptation of the devil by recourse to God's written Word. Jesus did not use the power that is His as the Son of God, but He used the resource available to Him as a son of man—the same resource available to each one of us.

20. As time permits, allow individuals to share.

21. *For personal reflection. Sharing optional.* As time permits, allow individuals to share their reflections on the wonder of our Savior, the God-man, Jesus.

22. Encourage participants to share insights they have gained through their study in the past week.

Listen Today and Believe

Hebrews 3:1–4:13

Preparing for the Session

Central Thought

The Word of God addresses us today; hearing it with faith leads to our entering the promised eternal rest.

Objectives

That participants, led by the Holy Spirit, will

1. understand the Spirit's warning to listen to the Gospel now in this "today" of opportunity;
2. earnestly yearn to enter the heavenly rest;
3. believe more firmly the Gospel message;
4. hear and heed the Gospel Word by weekly worship, daily Bible reading, and faithful study of the Bible with fellow Christians.

For the Small-Group Leader

Small-Group Discussion Helps

In Study 1 we considered that God has spoken. He spoke in the old times by the prophets. But in the new order of things it is Christ through whom and in whom God speaks. And that is the best revelation of all. In this week's study we hear the call of God to pay attention to this better—this best—message.

Day 1 • Hebrews 3:1–6

1. Verse 1 calls Jesus "the apostle and high priest." (a) In John 12:49 Jesus declares that He has been sent by God (that is, the Father) to speak God's message to the world. (b) According to 1 John 2:1–2, Jesus, as our High Priest, atones for us sinners and intercedes (speaks for) on our behalf before God the Father.

2. (a) Moses spoke for God. He told them about God's will revealed in the Ten Commandments. (b) Moses spoke for his people. On their behalf he pleaded for God's forgiveness for the sake of the promises that God had made to Abraham and the other patriarchs.

3. *Similarity*: Both Moses and Jesus were faithful in fulfilling the responsibilities given to them by God. *Difference*: Much greater honor is given to Jesus than to Moses. There is a vast difference between the apostleship and priestly function of Moses and that of Jesus. Moses was only a servant of God in His house; Jesus, however, is God's Son. Moses serves *within* God's kingdom. Jesus serves *over* God's house.

4. *Believers* in the Lord Jesus Christ.

Day 2 • Hebrews 3:7–19

5. The children of Israel in the Old Testament, specifically during the wilderness wandering after Moses led them from Egypt, didn't pay attention to God's message. In fact, they rebelled against that message more than once. (a) They assembled and refused to trust that God would provide needed water. (b) God was particularly displeased with such rebellion, because these same rebellious people had been witnesses to the miracles God performed in Egypt and in the wilderness to free and to sustain them. God finally lost patience with the Israelites when they refused to trust and obey Him by entering and taking possession of the land He had given them.

6. *For personal reflection. Sharing optional.* Allow any volunteer sharing, especially if thereby the participants are encouraged to comfort and encourage one another with the Good News of Jesus' forgiving love.

7. Discussion about those things that help us pay attention to God's message (Word and Sacrament, as found and experienced in church, Bible class, and private or family devotional life, or just plain pondering the "love of God which is in Christ Jesus" [Romans 8:39]) would be in order here. Sharing skills or experiences that have promoted more careful attention to God's message would be appropriate too.

Day 3 • Hebrews 4:1–7

8. (a) To enter the rest, the land of promise that God had picked out for them, the Israelites needed to receive God's promise with faith. (b) We also need to have faith in God's promise of grace through Jesus, our Savior, if we are to enter the rest that God is preparing for us.

9. We obtain this faith we need through hearing the message of the Gospel.

10. The crucial time to hear and believe the Gospel is right now, "Today"! Right now is the opportunity the Lord is giving to us to hear and believe the Gospel. How long this opportunity will go on no one can say.

11. Encourage participants to say how they are giving God an opportunity to produce and preserve faith in them by taking part in this and other Bible studies and readings, by attending worship, by personal or family devotions, and by giving attention to the Gospel at other times. We encourage this faith in others when we share the Gospel with them by telling them of God's love for them and particularly of how His love moved Him to provide a Savior from sin and eternal death.

Day 4 • Hebrews 4:8–11

12. Believers will rest from the weariness and frustrations that come from the imperfections, weaknesses, and sinfulness to which we are subject in this life (1 Corinthians 15:42–44), and from death and its grief and pain as they enjoy eternal pleasures in heaven (Revelation 21:4).

13. (a) The Sabbath taught the Israelites to look to God as the Creator of all that is and to acknowledge and worship Him alone as God. (b) The Sabbath taught the Israelites to look ahead to that time when God would give them rest from sin and death.

14. Complete rest is to be found only in the presence of God. We may rest our bodies and minds, but our spirits will still be restless until we have come to rest in God's presence through faith in Jesus as our Savior. Jesus invites us to come to Him and to find rest for our souls (Matthew 11:28–30).

15. Encourage participants to put this passage in their own words.

Day 5 • Hebrews 4:12–13

16. The writer urges us to pay more attention to the Gospel so that we do not drift away from the faith and God. He warns us that a day is coming when we must submit to the most scrutinizing judgment. We will not be able to slip by that judgment.

17. *Isaiah 55:10–11*: God's Word always accomplishes God's purpose and mission; it never fails to do His will. *Psalm 119:9, 11, 105, 130:* God's Word guides believers as they attempt to live according to God's will, giving light and understanding as to what God's will for us is. *2 Timothy 3:16–17*: The Scriptures instruct us in living a life that is righteous and fruitful with God-pleasing actions. *1 Peter 1:23*: Most important of all, the Holy Spirit uses the Word of the Gospel to give us a new birth and a new life by bringing us to faith in Jesus, our Savior.

18. Encourage participants to speak about how God's Word has been effective in their own lives. Most will be able to speak of the comfort and encouragement they have found in God's Word in times of crisis or sorrow. Others may tell how they found guidance in the Word of God. Some will speak of how God's Word has reproved them when they sinned and how God's Word refreshed them and gave them joy with its Gospel assurances and promises.

Our Great High Priest

Hebrews 4:14–6:20

Preparing for the Session

Central Focus

Draw near to God through Jesus, our High Priest, who has undergone suffering and death and has ascended and entered the heavenly temple.

Objectives

That participants, led by the Holy Spirit, will

1. understand how and why Jesus is our great High Priest;
2. desire to draw nearer to Jesus through faith;
3. be ready for solid food, that is, for a more mature understanding of God's Word concerning Jesus;
4. publicly confess Jesus as their Savior;
5. rely on Jesus as the anchor of their hope concerning God;
6. resolve to follow Jesus to the goal—the rest God has prepared for His people in heaven.

For the Small-Group Leader

Bible Background

As the topic shifts from word of revelation to deeds of salvation, the main points of comparison become the appointment and actions of Aaron and the Old Testament priests, on the one hand, and the earthly ministry, death, and ascension of Jesus' priestly work on the other. It is especially important at this point to review what the Old Testament has to say about the high priest, especially about his movements and actions on Yom Kippur, the great Day of Atonement (Leviticus 16).

The special calling and privilege of this divinely instituted office bearer should not be missed. Though the high priest is a man of sinful flesh himself, he is allowed, by God's command, to make sacrifice for himself and so be sanctified and consecrated. He becomes, by grace, an appointed mediator to approach the holy God on behalf of sinful people. By God's call and direction, the institution of the high priesthood was the final plank in a bridge over the gap between the holy God and the fallen, sinful world.

Picture it this way: when sin came, a chasm opened between the holy God and the sinful world. God would send His Son to cross that chasm and bridge that gap. To prophesy of and to prepare for the salvation He would provide, God called Israel, out of all the nations, to be "His" holy people. They were not sinless, but they were called to be a place of God's revelation and preparation for Jesus. In building a bridge between the sinful world and the holy God, they were a first plank in the revelation model. The true Israel was Christ. And within Israel, the Levites were a second plank, set aside for God. And within the Levites, the priests. And from within the priests, the high priest—a foreshadowing of the sinless mediator God would send. For the sake of revealing that grace of God in Jesus—and only for that sake—Israel was called, the Levitical order of priesthood was instituted, and the ritual of Yom Kippur was commanded.

The second element of Bible background to this lesson is from the New Testament Gospels, where Jesus' birth and Baptism (Jesus' installation into His office by God) are reported, where His prayers and intercessions are recorded, where His obedient suffering and death are described, and where His resurrection and ascension to God's throne in heaven are revealed. These are all connected to the priestly pattern of office and work.

Jesus is an apostle *to* us and a priest *for* us (Session 2). More to the point, Jesus is our High Priest, our *great* High Priest. There are elements about Him that make Him special and unique, our High Priest above and beyond any other priest.

Small-Group Discussion Helps

Day 1 • Hebrews 4:14–16

1. Jesus' transcendence is underscored in 4:14. He has "gone through the heavens" (the King James Version reads "passed into the heavens"). Ephesians 4:10 tells

us He "ascended higher than all the heavens, in order to fill the whole universe." It is because He has been so highly exalted that He is such a great High Priest. He is transcendent. One dictionary explains transcendent with words and phrases like "extraordinary," "superior," "supreme," and "going beyond ordinary limits." These certainly apply to Jesus. He is extraordinary: Jesus is unselfish, compassionate, loving, and full of power. He is superior: Jesus is the Son of God. He is supreme: Jesus is God. He goes beyond ordinary limits: Jesus performs miracles. Discuss other words students have found to define the word *transcendent* and how these fit to describe Jesus.

2. In 4:15 we are presented with the intriguing thought that Jesus was surrounded by the same circumstances and tempted with the same temptations and intensity as we are. That takes on meaning when we stop and ponder the temptations and the circumstances that assail us: peer pressure, opportunities for dishonesty, the tug of the flesh, the temptation to "just forget about God." Discussion here can give real meaning to the phrase "tempted in every way, just as we are," and, more important, to the Gospel message that there is strength for us from the Christ who knows what our temptations are like because He experienced them too and overcame them for us.

3. (a) We sometimes lightly trip over the word *grace* without sounding its depth or savoring its full flavor. Christ's grace became ours because of His self-sacrifice and denial (2 Corinthians 8:9). His grace is all-sufficient for us; we need nothing more (2 Corinthians 12:9). Grace *alone* saves us, not any good works we do. It's God who saves us by grace—and God who works in us to do good works (Ephesians 2:8–10). (b) and (c) Let participants share their personal responses of thanks and appreciation for God's grace.

Day 2 • Hebrews 5:1–10

4. Priests were to represent their people before God; specifically, priests were to offer the gifts and sacrifices to God that would atone for sin.

5. Jesus is like (though better than) the priests of old. Those high priests knew enough about sin firsthand to understand the sins and remorse of the people. After all, they too were sinners and needed to be forgiven and cleansed themselves before they could be channels of God's forgiveness and cleansing for those they were appointed to serve.

6. Jesus, too, has a firsthand acquaintance with the things in our life that reveal our weakness and dependency and bring us shame. He didn't sin, but He was up against all the weaknesses common to us, such as sorrow (Matthew 26:37–38), abandonment, betrayal (Matthew 26:43–45), rejection (John 7:5), and death (Philippians 2:8). He understands.

7. (a) Another point of comparison between Jesus and the priests of old is appointment. Just as Aaron and his successors held their office by God's appointment, (b) so Christ also was appointed to His priestly office by the Father's direct appointment.

Day 3 • Hebrews 5:11–6:3

8. (a) Participants will likely supply many distractions that prevent Christians from giving their full attention to God's Word—among them a lack of time, other responsibilities, worries, time-consuming interests, and a lack of energy. (b) Christians need to learn to order their time and set priorities so that they set aside time for reading and studying God's Word as a necessity for spiritual nourishment and Christian growth. No life is so full or busy that time cannot be found for God's Word.

9. (a) If Christians are to move off a "baby" level of Christianity, then they must first see that it is important and be motivated to do so. Christian growth toward spiritual maturity will take commitment and effort, and a Christian who sees no reason to make this commitment or the required effort is not likely to do anything. Kindly admonition, example, and pointing to the joy and beauty of God's love in Christ can be most encouraging. (b) Immature Christians will reveal their spiritual condition by immature behavior, including the behavior Paul found in the Corinthians—jealousy and quarreling. Spiritual immaturity also shows itself in such behavior as inability to receive admonition, unwillingness to yield to others, refusal to share with others, temper tantrums, insistence on being the center of attention, and other forms of childish behavior.

10. (a) Ignorance of what God's Word actually teaches will leave a Christian vulnerable to false teaching that claims to be Bible doctrine. How many have been mis-

led by such deceptions! When we do not know what God's Word actually teaches, we will be easily misled by those who may be sincere but wrong or who may even be spiritual charlatans. (b) Christians can guard against such deception by training themselves in what the Bible actually teaches. Steps toward this goal will include faithful attendance of the services of a church that teaches what God's Word teaches, participation in the Bible classes conducted by such a church, Bible reading, reading reliable Christian literature, and prayer for the guidance and blessing of the Holy Spirit. Encourage participants to recount how they have taken these steps. Participation in this LifeLight class is itself a giant step toward the goal of maturity!

11. (a) Christians believe the Gospel. To believe the Gospel they must know what it is. As Paul declares, "How can they believe in the one of whom they have not heard? And how can they hear without someone preaching to them?" (Romans 10:14). (b) But, as we see from Hebrews 6:1–3, God does not mean for Christians to remain on this basic, elementary level, but to grow and progress. How else will Christians be able to share the Gospel with others, to guard against error, and to advise and counsel one another in regard to the problems and perplexing conditions that come up in life? (c) Give an understanding and compassionate ear, along with wise, Bible-based counsel to people who are hurting; teach in Sunday school, VBS, and other congregational education efforts; and so forth.

Day 4 • Hebrews 6:4–12

12. (a) God wants all to be saved. He does not wish to deny His grace to anyone. It isn't God's refusal to forgive or to supply grace that damns the sinner. God's grace in Christ is for all. Christ went to the cross for all. Forgiveness has been won for all. (b) But someone who refuses to accept that pardon from Christ has refused the only means of pardon. Salvation is only available in Jesus; someone who will not have Jesus has turned away the one opportunity for forgiveness and salvation. It is the rejection of Christ that cuts one off from pardon.

13. God desires to welcome back repentant sinners, no matter how often they fall away and then return. So long as the repentance is real—so long as the sinner truly regrets the sin, desires to be forgiven, and earnestly means, with God's help, to live a better life—God is ready to receive that lost sinner back. (a) The son who "changed his mind" (repented) "did what his father wanted" and was accepted into the kingdom. (b) Jesus movingly pictures the heavenly Father's readiness to receive repentant sinners in the father's eagerness and joy to have his lost son back again in the parable of the prodigal or lost son. (c) In Romans 11:23 Paul writes of how God is ready to receive back again those Jews who had rejected Jesus as the Messiah and, by doing so, had been cut off from His people.

14. In Hebrews 6:7–8 we find a helpful illustration that makes clear the necessity of receiving the grace of God in Christ. This same basic point is made in Jesus' parable of the sower and the seed. In that parable Jesus speaks of those who hear His Word, accept it, and produce the crop of a God-pleasing life that honors and serves Jesus. Encourage participants to say how they are honoring and serving Jesus.

Day 5 • Hebrews 6:13–20

15. An oath confirms what is being said. Those who take an oath place themselves into the hands of one greater than themselves, submitting themselves to punishment if they are speaking falsely.

16. God wanted to make the certainty of the fulfillment of His promise very clear, so He confirmed His promise with an oath.

17. God's promise to all who believe is that they will enter His rest—His eternal, glorious kingdom.

18. As a result of God's promise confirmed with His oath, we have the hope of entering God's rest as an anchor for our souls. It is something on which we can depend, something that will uphold us.

Better and Forever

Hebrews 7

Preparing for the Session

Central Focus

Study of the Old Testament confirms that Jesus, High Priest according to the order of Melchizedek, is guarantor of a better testament, which introduces a better hope, through which we are drawing near to God.

Objectives

That participants, led by the Holy Spirit, will

1. understand that Jesus is the High Priest on whom they may rely for atonement and intercession before God;
2. be confident that God will always receive them when they come to Him through Jesus, since God has established Jesus' priesthood with an oath;
3. look to Scripture itself to interpret Scripture;
4. rely only on Jesus to bring them near to God.

For the Small-Group Leader

Bible Background

The Old Testament background for this lesson is brief and, for that very reason, often puzzling. Genesis 14:18–20 leaves many historical questions unanswered. As a result, many interpreters have filled in the gaps and tried to satisfy human curiosity.

One old line of Jewish interpretation identifies Melchizedek with Shem and says "the one true priesthood" was handed down from God to Adam, to Seth, to Noah, to Shem (Melchizedek), and so to Abraham, and through him to Levi and Aaron. Another actually finds a way to turn the Bible's words upside down: Abram actually blessed Melchizedek, they say. Both of these alternatives preserve the idea of the superiority of the Levitical priesthood.

Other students of ancient history surmise that Melchizedek was chieftain (priest-king) of a local Canaanite tribe, the Jebusites. They suggest that the incident is recorded later in order to raise the status of the cult (and Levitical priesthood) in Jerusalem by showing that even the patriarch Abraham once paid homage to the priest who was "King of (Jeru)Salem."

Jewish interpreters already have an assumption that becomes the guide in their interpretation: Scripture exalts the institutions of Judaism. And the historical interpreter likewise has an assumption: the origin of the materials in the text lies in the working out of this-worldly motives, conflicts, and processes.

The author of Hebrews, who is a good model for us on the subject of how to read the Old Testament, shows none of those assumptions. He has an assumption and a process all his own. For he is a believer in Jesus, the Son of God, the full and final revelation from God. And because of that, the Holy Spirit leads him to read the Old Testament quite differently. He looks at it and asks: How does this testify to Jesus? He knows the Old Testament is the Word of God, but he will not hear it teach anything that obscures the glory of Jesus. And he will not assume that its reports are the result of human will and motives. Nor will he fill in the gaps of what the Old Testament does not say in order to satisfy curiosity or give a "reasonable reconstruction."

Indeed, his interpretation is not "reasonable" (formed by reason); it is "spiritual" (taught by the Spirit). Staying with precisely what is said (and not said) in Genesis 14, adding Psalm 110:4 and everything he knows and believes about Jesus, he comes to the conclusion that God put Melchizedek in Abram's path that day, directed their encounter, and saw to it that the composition and preservation of the scriptural report of it would be in these precise words (verbal inspiration). This was in order to liken Melchizedek to Jesus, the Son of God, and reveal beforehand, in the Old Testament itself, the superiority of the priesthood of the coming Messiah.

Our writer isn't finished working through the notion that Jesus, our great High Priest, is above and beyond the ordinary, run-of-the-mill priesthood. He's already established that Jesus' priesthood is better. He is out to underscore that even more decidedly and to impress upon us, too, that Jesus and His priesthood on our behalf is endless and eternal.

Small-Group Discussion Helps

Day 1 • Hebrews 7:1–10

1. Two things, at least, made the priesthood of Melchizedek exceptional. He was a priest who bestowed on old father Abraham the blessing of God, and he received and accepted tithes from Abraham.

2. The writer of our New Testament letter to the Hebrews finds additional information in the account of this figure. (a) His name means "king (Melchi) of righteousness (Zedek)." (b) His title is "king of Salem" (in Hebrew, "peace"). (c) His family connections are unknown; he is not connected to a known human line of priests. He appears and disappears within the space of three verses, and yet—as later references to him make clear—Melchizedek was a significant Old Testament figure. (d) These details cause the writer to connect Melchizedek with Jesus. Jesus is the King from heaven, holy and righteous, who came to bring us peace with God through His redeeming work. As we shall see, the lack of a genealogy or of a priestly lineage also becomes an important connection with Jesus.

3. **Challenge question.** The writer is declaring that Melchizedek, because he has no predecessors or successors in his ministry, has an eternally living ministry. In this respect, Melchizedek prefigures Christ's own eternal, unending priesthood. Some Bible students believe that Melchizedek actually was Christ, who appeared to Abraham before His incarnation, or becoming man by being born of the Virgin Mary. The text itself, however, would seem not to support this point of view, since it says Melchizedek was "*like* the Son of God" (v. 3).

4. **Challenge question.** Two additional details of the account from Genesis are cited to show that Melchizedek was a priest superior to the Levitical priests, who served among the Israelites. (a) Melchizedek blessed the patriarch Abraham. The person in the superior position is always the one who gives the blessing; the person in the inferior position receives the blessing. (b) Furthermore, Abraham gave a tithe of his booty to Melchizedek and, by doing so, acknowledged him as his priest, his spiritual superior. And what Abraham did, he did not only for himself and in his own name, but for his descendants (including his great-grandson Levi, the ancestor of the Levitical priests) as well. Abraham was acknowledging Melchizedek as the spiritual superior of his Levite descendants.

Day 2 • Hebrews 7:11–14

5. The Law established and regulated the Levitical priesthood. Every important detail concerning the Levitical priesthood was set down in the Law given through Moses. Therefore, to change the priesthood required a change in regard to the Law itself. This change has, in fact, been made. God set aside the ceremonial regulations of the Law when they were fulfilled by Christ (v. 18).

6. Jesus could not have served as a priest under the regulations of the Law, because the Law restricted the priesthood to Levites, who were descendants of Aaron. Jesus was not of the tribe of Levi but of the tribe of Judah.

7. The writer has already shown that, while Jesus does not fit into the Levitical priesthood, He does match the priesthood of Melchizedek, which the writer has also shown to be superior to the Levitical priesthood.

8. The patriarch Jacob, when giving his dying blessing to his sons, prophesied that the scepter (symbol of kingship) would remain with the tribe of Judah until the Messiah came; the Messiah, or Christ, would reign forever as eternal King. This prophecy was fulfilled when, after the death of King Saul, who was from the tribe of Benjamin, God gave the kingship to David and to his descendants. Both David and Jesus were descended from Judah.

Day 3 • Hebrews 7:15–19

9. While Melchizedek himself disappeared, another in his priestly order has appeared to remain forever. His priesthood is not based on ancestry but on the fact that His life cannot be destroyed. This reflects Jesus' resurrection, that He sits at God's right hand, and that His priestly work is all-sufficient. This priest, who is in the order of Melchizedek, is Christ Jesus. Jesus is our High Priest forever.

10. What distinguishes the Melchizedek priesthood from the Levitical priesthood is that the Levitical priest-

hood was established on ancestry, but the Melchizedek priesthood was established on a life that cannot be ended.

11. The Law is useless since it cannot make us righteous or acceptable to God. It is too weak to do that, because it has no power of its own, and human nature is too weak to attain righteousness by it. Paul declares that the Law cannot do away with our sin but can only expose it for what it is and hold us accountable for it.

12. (a) Priests, descended from Levi and Zadok, were the only ones permitted to enter God's sanctuary and to serve Him by offering the required sacrifices. (b) Jesus' way allows, indeed enables, us to draw near to God. This phrase is one of the catch phrases of the letter and has been summarized by some with the phrases "listen," "draw near," and "hold on." (c) Jesus' way, in fact, *brings* us near to God. It removes our sin through the atoning power of the blood of Christ. (d) Jesus' way provides us with a sincere heart that approaches God with the full assurance of faith, which knows our consciences have been cleansed and our bodies washed through Holy Baptism.

Day 4 • Hebrews 7:20–22

13. (a) By sealing Jesus' priesthood with an oath, He gave the assurance that He will never change His mind but will always accept the atonement by which Jesus won our righteousness before God and the forgiveness of our sins. (b) How assuring to know that whatever sins we have committed, or however many times we have committed them, God will not go back on His promise to forgive and receive us for the sake of Jesus. Jesus' priestly ministry will always be great enough to remove our sins from God's sight!

14. God sealed His covenant with Abraham by an oath (Genesis 22:15–18). God sealed His covenant with the Israelites with an oath (Deuteronomy 29:1–2, 12–13). God also sealed with an oath His covenant with David (Acts 2:29–30).

15. In this thrilling passage from the conclusion of Romans 8, Paul expresses his conviction that nothing whatever will be able to separate us from the love of God in Jesus. How reassuring this is to us, particularly when facing obstacles and challenges that seem overwhelming. Encourage participants to read their personal statements of what it means to them that God has guaranteed their salvation through Christ.

Day 5 • Hebrews 7:23–28

16. The writer refers once again to the fact that the ministries of the Levitical priests were limited to their lifetimes; death ended their service. But Jesus' ministry continues forever, since He lives forever (Psalm 110:4).

17. As a consequence, Jesus will always be there to save those who look to Him, and He will always be able to intercede for those who come to Him.

18. Jesus is holy. There is no need for Him to make sacrifice to atone for His own sins. Jesus' priesthood is perfect and complete, in contrast to the weakness apparent in the priesthood of the Levites.

19. *Romans 12:1–2*: We sacrifice our way of life in this world, as we devote ourselves to obeying God, not following the ways of this world. *Philippians 4:18*: We sacrificially support the Lord's work, including gifts to the Lord's servants. *Hebrews 13:15–16*: We sacrificially serve as a result of our faith and our witness about Jesus and through the worship we give to Him and the service given to the Lord's kingdom and to our neighbors for the Lord's sake.

20. No sacrifice needs to be made to atone for sin, since Jesus' sacrifice was once for all. Christians do offer sacrifices to God, but these are sacrifices of thanksgiving and worship, not sacrifices of atonement. We "sacrifice" not in order to gain salvation, but because we are saved. "Therefore" in Romans 12:1 points to the preceding presentation of God's grace in Christ, the source of both our salvation and the new life we live in Him. All these are sacrifices that please God, since they flow from faith in Jesus, our Redeemer.

A New Covenant

Hebrews 8

Preparing for the Session

Central Focus

The priestly ministry of Christ, being better than the old covenant's priestly ministry, replaces it, even as the new covenant fulfills and takes the place of the old.

Objectives

That participants, led by the Holy Spirit, will

1. know and understand the covenant that God has established with them through Jesus;
2. trust only in Jesus as the Savior from all sin and as intercessor before God;
3. reject teachings that state that ceremonial regulations of the old covenant are still in force;
4. hear or read the Gospel daily to allow the Spirit to enter and work within their heart.

For the Small-Group Leader

Bible Background

There are two key Old Testament passages behind Hebrews 8. The first is Exodus 25:40 (Hebrews 8:5). Moses, about to construct the tabernacle, is warned: "See that you make them according to the pattern shown you on the mountain." When God spoke with Moses on Mount Sinai and gave him all the instructions about the tabernacle and its worship, He showed him the "pattern" or type or model for it, namely, the heavenly tabernacle of which this earthly one was to be a counterpart, an imitation. That little word *pattern*, in the single verse Exodus 25:40, is taken as scriptural evidence to support the existence of a heavenly sanctuary.

The other key passage is Jeremiah 31:31–34, which is quoted at length (Hebrews 8:8–12). This is a passage from the Old Testament writings that spoke of the new covenant the Lord planned to make. It would surpass the old covenant He had previously made. That covenant had been broken, and the people were about to be punished by being taken into exile. But the new covenant would be characterized by the forgiveness of sins and an indwelling of the will of God in the hearts of people. If there were any doubt that the old covenant was forward pointing and to be in effect only until the new covenant should come, this passage from Jeremiah should dispel it.

Further biblical materials employed in this lesson are from the sayings of Jesus concerning His mission and the Old Testament laws: Mark 2:18–22; Matthew 5:17–18; John 5:39; and also Paul's word in Romans 10:4: "Christ is the end [the goal] of the law [the old covenant]." The point extracted from the whole scriptural testimony on the subject is this: There is only one reason why God ordered things to be as they are in the Old Testament. That is to point forward to Jesus Christ. When He came, the new covenant was inaugurated and so everything about the forward-pointing old covenant was fulfilled and made obsolete, surpassed and displaced—in a word, replaced.

There is a progression in the writer's thought, a method in his presentation. We've moved from the message to the message bearer (the apostle) to the priest. In each case the point is that, as good as the original might have been, Jesus is better. His message is certainly better (Gospel as opposed to Law); His apostleship is better (of course, since the message His apostleship brought was Gospel as opposed to Law); and His priesthood was vastly better. Now we come to really good news. The new covenant is better, much better than the old.

Small-Group Discussion Helps

Day 1 • Hebrews 8:1–2

1. Jesus is the High Priest we need, since He lives eternally in heaven right next to the Father's throne, where He speaks on our behalf. He has atoned fully for all. Since we are sinners, whose sinful human nature continues to involve us in sin, we need the forgiveness and grace He offers to us.

2. The "sanctuary, the true tabernacle" is heaven—the presence of God.

3. *For personal reflection. Sharing optional.* As our heavenly intercessor, Jesus obtains our forgiveness and preserves us in faith so that we will not be lost due to the attacks of the devil or of the unbelieving world around us. Jesus' High Priestly Prayer for the disciples and for all believers, recorded in John 17, tells us what Jesus asks for as He intercedes for us. Our eternal salvation is Jesus' great concern (and should be ours as well).

Day 2 • Hebrews 8:3–5

4. The writer refers to the duty of a high priest to offer sacrifices and gifts to God to atone for the sins of the people. These sacrifices were of animals, whose blood God used to cleanse the Israelites.

5. The Levitical priests offered the blood of various kinds of animals to make atonement for the sins of the Israelites. As our great High Priest, Jesus offered His own precious blood as atonement for our sins.

6. The fact that their tabernacle was a copy of the true tabernacle in heaven should have caused the Israelites to look beyond it in faith to the true tabernacle, just as Abraham looked beyond Canaan to the true promised land of heaven.

7. The earthly copy of the true tabernacle was made by human hands, although according to a pattern given from heaven. The true tabernacle was created directly by God, without human involvement.

8. Not only the tabernacle but the form of worship conducted in connection with it, the Sabbath and the Jewish festivals, the dietary regulations—in fact, all of the ceremonial regulations given in the Old Testament—were a shadow cast backward by the coming reality: the Christ and the atonement He would make for sins.

9. The worship of heaven will center around Jesus. It will honor and praise Him as the Redeemer and will be done with music and song—just like our worship here.

Day 3 • Hebrews 8:6–9

10. Jesus' priesthood is superior to that of the Levitical priests, because Jesus' priesthood makes us holy, is backed up by God's own oath, is permanent, and atoned for all sins once and for all.

11. The new covenant is founded upon better promises than the first covenant.

12. The essence of the first covenant of God with His people, the Old Testament covenant, was, "Obey Me, and I will be your God and you will be My people. Walk in all the ways I command you, that it may go well with you" (Jeremiah 7:23).

13. (a) God Himself was the active agent in this covenant. He initiated it, and He promised His blessing to those who live in it. (b) The Israelites were to fulfill the terms of the covenant by obeying God and following His commands.

14. Instead of obeying God and following His commands, the Israelites were unfaithful to God. They would not listen to the Lord or submit to Him. They insisted on walking in their own counsels.

15. When the first covenant failed, God made a new covenant, one that would not depend on the obedience or righteousness of those who lived in it but on the obedience and righteousness of Christ. This covenant was intended by God from the time sin entered the world and was promised through Jeremiah.

16. God brought this new covenant into effect "when the time had fully come" by sending Jesus into this world as a human being, under obedience to the Law to redeem sinners.

Day 4 • Hebrews 8:10–11

17. God would put His laws into the hearts of people. That is, God would make the people to be attuned to His ways.

18. This new element is fulfilled in Christians as God gives His Holy Spirit to us. The Spirit creates a new person within us—a new person who desires to live as God desires (Romans 8:5–9). God fills the hearts of Christians with love, causing them to keep the Commandments out of love for others (Romans 13:8–10). In addition to love, the Spirit produces in believers many other godly qualities, some of which Paul lists in Galatians 5:22–23.

19. So much is the Spirit working within them that Christians are not always conscious of how they are responding to the Spirit's promptings. It seems natural and self-evident that they should do God's will. This

is evident in the response of those who, on Judgment Day, are surprised that their simple acts of love were really fulfilling the will of God so wonderfully by being done for Jesus Himself!

20. The credit for the good deeds and God-pleasing actions of Christians goes entirely to God the Holy Spirit, who prompts and empowers Christians to do them. The God-pleasing lives of Christians are evidence of the Spirit's work within them.

21. God affirms of those who live under this new covenant that He is their God and they are His people.

22. With each person who lives within this covenant the Lord has a personal relationship. The Lord knows each of His people individually, and Christians know their Lord personally and hear and follow His voice (John 10:14, 27). Those who live in this covenant have a direct knowledge of and communication with the Lord. We live with God on familiar terms, with no human go-between needed (Hebrews 8:11).

23. Encourage participants to share their own sense of closeness to God and the awareness of His presence in their lives.

Day 5 • Hebrews 8:12–13

24. Best of all, God would remember our sins no more. (This is so fantastic and comprises such overwhelmingly good news that some note should be made of it, even if it is just a moment of silence while each member of your small group contemplates what that means to him or her.)

25. Encourage participants to indicate why the forgiveness of sins is important to them personally. The forgiveness of sins removes the barrier between us and God, permits God to be present with us and to bless us, and opens the doors of eternal life in heaven to us. How wonderful—and what a great relief!—to know that our sins—all of them!—have been forgiven.

26. Now that God has established the new covenant, the first covenant has become obsolete. It is of no practical relevance to us except to point to Christ and to trace God's loving plan to save us.

27. All of the ceremonial regulations of the first covenant have been abolished. They certainly have no relevance any longer to our relationship with God except a negative relevance if we insist that keeping them is necessary. In that case, they stand in the way of our relationship with God, since then we deny that Christ has fulfilled the Law and won salvation for us on the cross.

28. Every man-made religion ultimately makes salvation—our relationship with God—depend in whole or in part on our works, our goodness, our "doing." In the only true religion, God, not mankind, is the active agent. In the new covenant everything is in God's hands. He attunes us to His ways. He is God and master. He forgets our guilt for Jesus' sake. And the list goes on. Always God acts; He does for us what we are unable to do for ourselves. It is this thought, the climax to the writer's catalog of "betters," that sends us out today and every day with a song in our hearts and a wish to do God's will on earth as the angels do above.

Draw Near

Hebrews 9:1–10:18

Preparing for the Session

Central Focus

Jesus' ministry fulfills and replaces the forward-pointing ministry conducted by the Levitical priests in the earthly tabernacle. To trust and believe in Him means to draw near to God by the way opened up through His ministry.

Objectives

That participants, led by the Holy Spirit, will

1. know that Christ has fulfilled the Old Testament regulations fully;
2. regard the ceremonial regulations of the Old Testament as no longer applicable in our relationship to God;
3. trust in Christ alone as the atonement for all sin;
4. draw near to God through faith in Christ.

For the Small-Group Leader

Bible Background

A basic familiarity with the floor plan of the Israelite's ("earthly") tabernacle (and temple) and the regulations for the activities of the Levitical priests and of the high priest is essential if we are to understand the assertions made in this section of Hebrews. The instructions for constructing the ark of the covenant and the tabernacle are in Exodus 25–26.

Critical verses are 26:31–35, which describe the veil and the division of the tabernacle's interior space into the "Holy Place" and the "Most Holy Place." Verse 33 emphasizes that the function of the veil was to separate the Most Holy Place from the rest of the tabernacle.

Some of the daily activities of Aaron and his sons are described in Exodus 29:38–30:8: the morning and evening sacrifice of lambs at the altar and the burning of incense and trimming of the lamps inside the Holy Place. Further examples of ministrations for rites of purification are in Leviticus 14–15.

Leviticus 16 describes how only the high priest was to go into the Most Holy Place once a year with a bull whose blood would make atonement for his own sin and a goat to make atonement for the sins of the people. These actions and spaces in the earthly tabernacle have some special revelatory significance, as Hebrews 9 will make clear.

Small-Group Discussion Helps

All the writer's comparisons have culminated in the happy discovery that there is a new covenant between God and His people and that the new covenant is better than the original. It follows, therefore, that we ought to settle ourselves under this new covenant and cling to it with everything we've got.

"Draw near," the writer says. The idea is timely, even today. Pull up next to this better covenant. "Hold unswervingly." Or, to put it in a way that may, perhaps, seem more up-to-date, "Hang on!" Once you lay hold of this new relationship with God, don't let it slip away.

These are the key phrases as we study Hebrews 9:1–10:18. Draw near. There is even something of a giddiness about it, like riding a roller coaster. This new covenant is sheer delight. You don't know where it will take you. It will be exciting. It will be safe, too, since it's all God's doing. So hang on. Here we go!

Day 1 • Hebrews 9:1–10

1. (a) The first room was called the Holy Place. In this room were the lampstand and the table for the consecrated bread (showbread). The writer places the incense altar in the Most Holy Place, although it actually stood in the Holy Place (Exodus 40:1–5), since incense was also burned inside the Most Holy Place on the Day of Atonement (Leviticus 16:12–13). Only priests might enter the Holy Place. There are various interpretations of this seeming difficulty about the location of the altar of incense. R. C. H. Lenski postulates, "The golden altar of incense stood in the Holy Place, close to the veil; when offering the incense the priest faced the Mercy-

seat behind the veil; the incense was offered to God as being present at the Mercyseat" (*The Interpretation of the Epistle to the Hebrews and of the Epistle of James* [Minneapolis: Augsburg Publishing House], pp. 280–81).

Luther gives reasons for an altar in both the Holy Place and the Most Holy Place; or, alternatively, that "the censer was in the Holy of Holies, since it belonged there and was brought there by the priest on the Feast of the Atonement" from its normal place in the Holy Place (*Lectures on Titus, Philemon, and Hebrews*, Luther's Works, American edition: vol. 29 [St. Louis: Concordia Publishing House, 1968], p. 205).

Some relevant texts to check include Leviticus 16:12–13; Exodus 40:1–5; 1 Kings 6:22. At any rate, there is no pressing need to discuss the matter at length in the discussion group. (b) The Most Holy Place contained the ark of the covenant. Only the high priest might enter the Most Holy Place and only on the Day of Atonement.

2. The ark of the covenant contained a gold jar of manna, Aaron's staff, and the two stone tablets on which God had written the Ten Commandments. All of these objects were from the time of the exodus, when God had led Israel out of Egypt (Aaron's rod), marvelously preserved them (the manna), and made a covenant with them at Sinai (the stone tablets). The events of which these items were tokens reminded the Israelites of how God had come and dwelt among them and brought them to the Promised Land.

3. Jesus, as true man and true God, is present everywhere. He exercises His divine power especially for His church, His people, whom He promises to be with in a very special way, assuring us of His sustaining power and peace as we serve people in His name.

4. The high priest brought blood into the Most Holy Place. He sprinkled the blood on the gold cover over the ark of the covenant to make atonement for his own sins and for the sins of the people.

5. The restrictions concerning entrance into the temple, and particularly into the Most Holy Place, revealed that sin still prevented people from coming into the presence of God. People came direct access to God only when Jesus would come to remove the sin that separates people from God.

6. Now that our sin has been removed, we may approach God directly in our prayers and worship. We need no human mediator, since Jesus has made us acceptable to God. Encourage participants to express themselves in their own words.

Day 2 • Hebrews 9:11–22

7. Jesus entered this tabernacle bearing His own blood, by which He had obtained our eternal redemption.

8. The blood and ashes of animals cleansed worshipers outwardly, that is, by making them ceremonially clean. But the blood of Jesus cleanses our consciences by removing our sin forever and making us holy and righteous before God.

9. Christ's death is called a ransom because it has freed us from the guilt and power of sin at the cost of Christ's life.

10. (a) Jesus' blood was necessary for the establishment of a new covenant. A will, or testament, goes into effect only after a death has occurred. The old covenant required the death of sacrificial animals. The new covenant required the death of Jesus. Now that His death has occurred, we may enjoy the terms of the testament. (b) Jesus' death was necessary for the forgiveness of sins, since sin requires atonement made through the shedding of blood and the giving of life. Animal sacrifices were inadequate, incomplete, and imperfect, especially when compared to Christ's` full, clean, perfect sacrifice. Without the shedding of blood there can be no forgiveness. Jesus has made that forgiveness possible.

Day 3 • Hebrews 9:23–28

11. **Challenge question:** Copies (or shadows) and realities are parallels we find frequently in this section of Hebrews. (a) The Levitical priests foreshadowed the eternal priesthood of Christ. (b) The Law, or first covenant, foreshadowed the new covenant. (c) The earthly tabernacle was a copy of the heavenly tabernacle. (d) The animal sacrifices foreshadowed the once-for-all sacrifice of Jesus.

12. Hebrews 9:27 certainly rules out any idea of reincarnation, declaring that we die in this world only once. What happens next is not another life in this world, but life either in heaven or hell, depending on the outcome of the judgment. Believers are guaranteed eternal life in heaven. Unbelievers will spend eternity in hell. (b) We

live in this world only once. Now is our opportunity to serve God (John 9:4). Now we have a never-to-be-repeated opportunity to receive the redemption Jesus has won for us. Now is the time to hear and believe the Gospel. We will have no second chance once this life has been lived (2 Corinthians 6:1–2).

13. When we think of our sins and imperfections, the thought of facing God's judgment might cause us to feel terror and panic. But the Lord assures us that He has removed our sins and that we have nothing to fear from God's judgment so long as we cling to Jesus as our Redeemer. With faith in Christ we may face the judgment confidently and joyfully. Allow volunteers to share their feelings.

14. As time permits, encourage sharing. Psalm 16:11—Joy and eternal pleasure at God's right hand. Romans 8:29–30—Being like Jesus; glorified. 1 Corinthians 15:47–52—Being like Jesus; imperishable. 2 Corinthians 3:18—Transformed to be like Jesus, with ever-increasing glory. Philippians 3:20–21—Transformed body. 1 John 3:2–3—Being like Jesus, as we see Him as He actually is.

Day 4 • Hebrews 10:1–10

15. (a) The purpose of the sacrifices was not to remove sin but to reveal it and to be a continuing reminder of its reality. (b) Paul tells us that the Law itself had the same purpose. The Law could not do away with sin; it could only reveal it and show it for what it is.

16. (a) Still today we need the continual reminder of the reality of sin and its presence in our own lives, lest we begin to think we do not really need a Savior from sin or that sin is not so serious as to separate us from God eternally. Being reminded of sin is not pleasant and does not make us feel good, but it is vitally important to us that we know of it so that we will desire its removal. (b) Reminding people about sin does not do any good unless we also tell them of how God has removed our sin through the atonement made by Jesus on His cross. We must tell and remind people that God has done away with sin. (c) Many practical applications to life can come as participants share their answers. No doubt participants will identify the kind of "holier than thou" condemnatory and judgmental pointing to sins that they have felt or even have practiced. Or some "restore gently" experiences that come from the realization that all of us are subject to the same temptations we condemn in others. Note the "brothers" at the beginning of the Galatians text. When we realize that we're dealing with brothers and sisters in the faith, we're able to be kind and helpful, yet also truthful, in our admonitions.

Day 5 • Hebrews 10:11–18

17. Old Testament priests had to repeat sacrifices over and over. Those sacrifices were never totally satisfying or effective. Thus the priests stood, ready always to repeat the sacrifice. Jesus, however, made the perfect, once-for-all sacrifice. It never needed to be repeated or amended. Thus He could sit, and does, at God's right hand.

18. As the Joshua text indicates, the language here refers to the custom of indicating complete and final victory by placing one's foot on the neck of one's prostrate enemy. The enemy is the old evil foe, the devil, who holds the "power of death" over all who, like him, have sinned and deserve God's eternal punishment (Hebrews 2:14). On the Last Day, for which Christ now waits, death will be finally overcome and the devil will finally and irrevocably be cast into hell. Christ's rule will be fully evident to all.

19. The Bible here clearly states that it is the product of the Holy Spirit, who worked through the prophets, evangelists, and apostles. As Peter says, "Prophecy never had its origin in the will of man, but men spoke from God as they were carried along by the Holy Spirit" (2 Peter 1:21).

20. There is no further sacrifice for sin because no further sacrifice for sin is needed. Jesus' one sacrifice of Himself on the cross has fully atoned for the sins of all for all time.

21. Encourage participants to share which passage or section of the reading for this week meant the most to them and why.

Now Faith Abides

Hebrews 10:19–12:2

Preparing for the Session

Central Focus

On our pilgrimage, we should hold fast to our confession unwaveringly to the end, being strengthened to endure by a faith that looks upward to Jesus and forward to the heavenly goal.

Objectives

That participants, led by the Holy Spirit, will

1. have a clearer understanding of the nature and character of faith;
2. value the faith God has given to them by the work of the Spirit through the Gospel;
3. resolve to claim God's help in preserving, nourishing, and increasing faith in Jesus as the Savior from sin and only way to God;
4. encourage fellow Christians to stay faithful to Jesus.

For the Small-Group Leader

Bible Background

Hebrews 11, one of the most beloved chapters in the Bible, speaks about faith and provides many illustrations of the power and character of faith, beginning with Genesis and continuing through incidents from the intertestamental period. It presents a host of well-attested heroes of faith from Bible times.

A reference Bible will note the key Old Testament passage behind a particular verse (e.g., Genesis 4:4 for Hebrews 11:4 or Joshua 6:20 for Hebrews 11:30). But here are four selected passages, all of them referenced in Hebrews 11, that say something special about the nature of faith.

First, reread the account of Noah in Genesis 6:5–22. The words *faith* and *believe* are not actually found in that text. But note how aptly Hebrews 11:7 summarizes what is going on.

Noah's obedience rose out of his faith. *Before* the ark-construction command, God showed him grace (*favor*, Genesis 6:8); also *before* the unseen was revealed God declared Noah to be righteous (Genesis 6:9). God told righteous Noah of His plan (Genesis 6:13) and gave him precepts to prepare the ark. So Noah did what God commanded (Genesis 6:22). It is God who offered him grace, who declared him righteous, who gave him instructions. Noah obeys God. Noah's obedience followed his reception of God's favor. His action to build follows God's action to justify him. His obedience is a result of his acceptance of God's favor and is not the cause of God's grace. Noah's reaction to God's revelation did not cause him to be declared righteous and favored by God. Rather, by faith he received the righteousness God gave.

Second, consider Abraham and the command to sacrifice Isaac in Genesis 22. Abraham had been promised many descendants and had been told, "It is through Isaac that your offspring will be reckoned" (Genesis 21:12). In Isaac, not another subsequent substitute! For Abraham to be ready to give Isaac back to God through sacrifice and yet to believe God would fulfill His promise means that he believed God was able to raise the dead (Hebrews 11:19). When the ram was substituted for Isaac and Abraham got Isaac back, so to speak, from the dead, Abraham's faith was vindicated.

Third, Moses was led to leave his position as the son of Pharaoh's daughter and to identify himself with the Israelites and share in their ill treatment (Exodus 2:10; 5:1; Hebrews 11:24–26). This, which Moses did in faith and in obedience to the call of God, Hebrews calls "disgrace for the sake of Christ" (11:26).

Finally, the incidents referred to in verses such as Hebrews 11:35 are not all clear. The women who "received back their dead, raised to life again," could include the widows whose sons Elijah and Elisha raised (1 Kings 17:22; 2 Kings 4:35). But contrasted with them are others who suffered torture and were killed, refusing to take the easy way out. They believed in a better resurrection, into the life of the age to come, not back into this life. This could be referring to a well-known story of a Jewish woman and her seven sons who were all put to death for their faith under the Seleucid persecutions of the Jews in the second century B.C. The incident is recorded in 2 Maccabees 7, and you are encouraged to read about it in the Old Testament Apocrypha. (A copy, included in some Bibles, may be located in your church library or another library.)

Small-Group Discussion Helps

Faith has become the keyword in the discussion that compares the old and inadequate with the new, the all sufficient. The old message, the old messengers, the old Promised Land, the old priests and the old covenant, all are inferior to the new. There is a new and better message. The new promised land is not made with human hands but with the hands of God. The old priestly orders don't compare with our great High Priest, Jesus Christ. And the covenant that makes us the children of God—how utterly better it is than the covenant of old!

So draw near. Your faith makes you whole, makes you heirs in the new covenant. Let's turn our attention to this well-known and remarkable chapter on faith.

Day 1 • Hebrews 10:19–25

1. The writer summarizes what he has said regarding the new way God has opened through the work of Christ as our High Priest. (a) In verses 19–20 the writer says that we, with our prayers and worship, now may enter God's presence directly, and we will enter heaven when God calls us out of this life. We need no human mediators, because Jesus has opened heaven to us by the atonement He made with His death on the cross. (b) In verse 21 the writer refers to Jesus as the great High Priest, who saves and rules the church, which includes all who believe in Him.

2. The five exhortations—statements of encouragement—are to this effect: (a) Let's come to God confidently, in faith, since (*basis*) He, through Holy Baptism, has cleansed us from our sins, and God has opened heaven to us through Jesus, our great High Priest (vv. 19–21). (b) Let's keep believing in Christ as our Savior, trusting in God to give us strength to do so. The basis is the faithfulness of God in keeping His promises. (c) Let's think how we might encourage all of our fellow Christians to continue in Christian love and service. The unstated basis is the need for that encouragement. (d) Let's continue to worship God together regularly. The basis is the tendency to stop worshiping God. (e) Let's continue to encourage and help one another. The basis is the approaching day of the Lord's second coming and the judgment that will follow. Allow participants to say in their own words, to the best of their ability, what these texts are saying.

3. Our Baptisms are a source of encouragement to us when we realize that through them God has washed us from our sins, made us His own dear children, and lives with us in a covenant that He will never cancel. In terms of Romans 6, as paraphrased in the Small Catechism, Baptism "indicates that the Old Adam in us should by daily contrition and repentance be drowned and die with all sins and evil desires, and that a new man should daily emerge and arise to live before God in righteousness and purity forever."

Day 2 • Hebrews 10:26–31

4. It is important that participants understand this section properly. This section does not mean that God will grow tired of forgiving us or that there is a limit to God's grace. So long as we repent and trust in Christ as our Savior from sin, God's grace will be there for us, in this life and at the Day of Judgment. John assures us that if we acknowledge our sins and look to Christ for our atonement, the Lord will surely forgive any and all of our sins.

5. The writer is referring in this section to the sin of rejecting Christ as our Savior, of turning away from faith in Him, of denying that He is our Lord and Redeemer from sin. This is the sin of apostasy, of rejecting Jesus after having once believed in Him.

6. Someone who commits the sin of apostasy is left without hope, since there is only one way of salvation—through faith in Jesus. Apart from Him there is no forgiveness of sin, no shield from God's wrath against sin. No one may come to God except through Jesus. Commenting on Hebrews 10:26–31, the perceptive Bible scholar Martin Franzmann notes some people as foolish to believe they can deliberately sin and later repent only to sin again. He says, "Such sinning is the last step on the way toward apostasy; it is the expression of an 'evil unbelieving heart' (3:12)" (*The Word of the Lord* Grows [St. Louis: Concordia Publish-

ing House, 1961], p. 246). Such deliberate sinning is to purposefully cut off one's self from God, the giver of repentance and provider of forgiveness. Apostasy is worse than ignorance and unbelief (2 Peter 2:20–22). Apostasy is a total falling away (Hebrews 6:6), a total attitude (Hebrews 10:26) of one who personally crucifies Christ (Hebrews 6:6) a second time and thus aligns himself or herself with Christ's original crucifiers. This rules out fresh repentance, for they trample the Son of God under foot (Hebrews 10:29). God appeals, but they continually reject (Matthew 23:37).

7. Certainly every Christian will want to avoid the sin of apostasy, of rejecting Christ as Savior. God will keep us faithful to Him as we remain in or return to the covenant God established with us in Baptism and as we continue to hear and believe the Gospel. This is why we attend worship services frequently and regularly, why we take part in Bible classes and read the Scriptures, and why we remain in a Christian fellowship.

Day 3 • Hebrews 10:32–39

8. Some of the Hebrews who first received this letter had been persecuted because of their faith in Jesus. Some were insulted, lost their property, or were imprisoned (vv. 33a, 34b). Others stood up for them and were willing to be identified with those who were persecuted, even when this meant they might well receive the same ill treatment (vv. 33b, 34a).

9. Perhaps some of the participants in your discussion group will be able to relate a time when they suffered in some way because of their faith in or loyalty to Christ. Others may remember when they stood up for others who were ill treated and identified themselves with them publicly. They may remember that, though this experience was difficult and frightening at the time, they were strengthened as a result of it.

10. The lesson they learned was that God stood by them and did not abandon them but strengthened and rescued them. He will surely do so again.

11. (a) The writer refers to the time when Christ will come again in glory and power at the end of this age and will raise all the dead. All will face judgment. (b) The realization of Christ's second coming and the Day of Judgment will warn us not to fall away from Christ and will encourage us to stand firm in our faith, knowing that our steadfastness will one day be affirmed and rewarded.

Day 4 • Hebrews 11:1–19

12. This is a wonderful definition of faith. Faith is the certainty that what God promises is true, even if we cannot prove it or see any evidence that it is true.

13. While the magnitude, the orderliness and precision, and the beauty of the universe around us testify to the Creator, we cannot prove that God created the world around us in six days, as the Bible states. No one was there to observe the creation. This is where faith comes in, declaring, "God says it; therefore, I believe it."

14. Answers to this question, of course, will vary. Let the discussion emphasize how, in each case, it was God who provided the basis for the person's faith in His steadfast love.

15. Let participants share their thoughts. Some possibilities: (a) "This is crazy! I don't even know where I'm going. How will I know the people are friendly? What if there are bandits on the way?" (b) "Maybe God's made a mistake and we should try for an heir with a younger woman." (See Genesis 16:1–4.) "Maybe my servant should be my heir." (See Genesis 15:2–3.) (c) "Was it really God who spoke to me? What if I disobey God just this one time? After all, He is asking for a lot!"

16. Unless someone volunteers a comment, skip over this personal reflection question.

Day 5 • Hebrews 11:20–12:2

17 and 18. Encourage participants to tell of someone whose faith has been or is an example of faith to them.

19. It will be interesting and edifying to hear participants share their answers, noting also whether they choose Bible-times or contemporary Christian loved ones who have gone before. Emphasize the joy of being with all God's saints as we worship and praise Christ, our King!

20. Jesus Himself was looking forward also to the reason for which He came into the world—to redeem us from sin and death through His own death and resurrection. When Jesus completed that task, the Father seated Him once again at His own right hand, adding glory and honor for what He had accomplished to the glory that has been His from all eternity.

The Unshakable Kingdom

Hebrews 12:3–29

Preparing for the Session

Central Focus

Endure through difficulties, for you have received the unshakable kingdom; give thanks, therefore, and worship God.

Objectives

That participants, led by the Holy Spirit, will

1. recognize that the way of a Christian pilgrim is not easy but may well be lined with many hardships and suffering for Jesus' sake;
2. be willing to receive hardship and difficulty as a form of discipline sent by the Lord to strengthen and train His people;
3. regard the coming of the end of this age with confidence and joy, knowing they live in an unshakable kingdom;
4. hold on to the faith and values that are theirs in Christ, rejecting every temptation to trade in spiritual treasures for the temporary pleasures of this passing world;
5. give thanks to God for His unshakable kingdom.

For the Small-Group Leader

Bible Background

Four Old Testament passages figure prominently in this section, where we continue to find the Old Testament references underlying the earnest pleas of this New Testament letter. We also continue to find a pattern familiar to us in this letter: the new continues, contrasts with, and surpasses the old.

Hebrews 12:5–11 draws several conclusions from Proverbs 3:11–12. Two points from the Proverbs passage are very important. The first is that the passage is addressed to a "son." (Following the practice of that time, the Teacher of Wisdom addresses his student as "son.")

The other point is that discipline is an essential part of teaching. The repeated references to "discipline" (vv. 6–11) and the phrase "harvest of righteousness and peace" (v. 11) might also bring to mind another Old Testament passage, Isaiah 53. There the punishment that brings us peace is laid on God's Son (the Servant). The discipline laid on God's Son restores us to wholeness. Hebrews 5:8 told us that the Son "learned obedience from what He suffered." Putting all of this together, we see that Jesus, God's Son, is our forerunner (12:3) also in receiving the discipline God lays on His children.

A section with a number of phrases from Old Testament passages, Hebrews 12:12–17 concludes with a reference to Esau. We learn from Genesis 25:33–34; 27:30–40 how, in a weary moment, Esau gave up something that would be very valuable to him in the future in exchange for a single meal, which would satisfy his present, temporary physical desires. (While Esau could not later undo the fact that Isaac gave the firstborn's blessing to Jacob, this does not mean that Esau could not be saved by faith in Jacob's descendant, Jesus.)

The description of events at Mount Sinai in Hebrews 12:18–21 is dependent on Deuteronomy 4–5 and Exodus 19. Review those chapters. Note that Hebrews emphasizes how fearful and awe-inspiring the scene was to the observers.

Finally, the concluding encouragement (Hebrews 12:25–29) rests on an image in Haggai 2:6, in which the great day of the Lord's judgment and victory is called a day when "I will once more shake the heavens and the earth." All things of this creation will then be removed. Only what God has given and which belongs to the world to come will remain: His kingdom, which shall not fall when the Day of Judgment comes.

Small-Group Discussion Helps

As we emulate the cloud of witnesses in chapter 11 and Jesus, the pioneer and perfecter of our faith (12:1–2), we will run headlong—as they did—into trouble, just because we are faithful to God. The people cited in chapter 11 comprise "a great cloud of witnesses." Like those witnesses, we, too, must endure the cross, scorning the shame.

Day 1 • Hebrews 12:3–4

1. Jesus "endured the cross, scorning its shame" (v. 2). Included in what Jesus endured was an unjust and rough arrest, Matthew 26:55–56; physical and verbal abuse, 26:67–68; flogging, 27:26; public humiliation and more physical abuse, 27:27–31; insults by passersby, 27:39–41; and a cruel and torturous death, including the pain of abandonment by His heavenly Father, 27:46–50.

Day 2 • Hebrews 12:5–13

2. Readers are encouraged to remember that suffering or hardship is not to be regarded as an expression of the Lord's indifference or vengeance. It always has a positive, upbuilding purpose. Such experiences discipline us; they teach and train us to look to God with faith and hope, confident of His strengthening and deliverance. Such experiences are actually proof that the Lord loves and cares enough for us to train us in this way.

3. (a) Discipline is a sign of sonship, an indication that we are the sons and daughters of God. Verse 7 says it plainly, "God is treating you as sons. For what son is not disciplined by his father?" (b) The writer even insists that discipline is personally productive. No one wants to hear that, but it was a pertinent and practical point for those to whom this letter was written, who were suffering persecutions for their faith. And it has practical implications for our day. The kingdom of heaven, so the references maintain, comes to us down roadways often marked by hardship.

4. We have received the Holy Spirit, who lives in our hearts, strengthening us and keeping us in faith (John 14:16–17). In Baptism we have received a "new self," recreated in the image of God (Ephesians 4:24). "Like father, like son"—as children of God through faith in the Son, we become more like our holy Father as we yield to His discipline and to His Spirit (2 Corinthians 3:18; 2 Peter 1:4). What a fantastic and wonderful vision and reality, which strengthens us to "hold on" in the midst of any persecution!

5. We would not want to overstate the difficulties we sometimes endure because of our Christian faith. Nevertheless, some time may be well invested in having group members name some of the things they have had to endure because of their Christian convictions and how these have actually resulted in good.

6. **Challenge question.** We sometimes try to encourage people who complain because of their difficulties, saying, "Buck up!" or "Pull yourself together!" The writer is exhorting his readers to gather their strength to meet their hardships. He also tells them to live upright, moral lives that will help, and not hinder, their own efforts and the efforts of others to meet hardship with courage and strength. The most important word in the exhortation is *therefore*, which provides the motivation and power to do what the exhortation asks. It refers back to all of chapter 11 and especially to such Gospel reminders as verses 2–3 of this chapter. Jesus and what He did for us—and what He does for us by giving us His Spirit—makes the difference between secular advice and Christian exhortation. Without the *therefore* of God's love in Christ, all exhortations are pure moralism, doomed to failure. With Christ, we are heartened and empowered to live boldly the new life in Him.

Day 3 • Hebrews 12:14–17

7. (a) The Bible insists that Christians live in peace with all people, starting with our fellow Christians. There is so little identification of Christianity with peacemaking. Could that be because the world sees very little peacemaking among Christians? Scripture suggests that insisting on our "rights" take second place to our efforts to live at peace, in harmony, in love with all, starting with our brothers and sisters in the faith. Romans 14:19–21 underscores that principle in connection with the disputes about eating nonkosher food. The underlying concern is for the fellow Christian, so that no dissension may keep anyone from turning away from Christ. Strife among Christians is a great offense against the unbelievers, weakening our witness to them about the love of Christ. (b) The goal of our relationship with God is holiness. Jesus died to make us holy before God, and now, because of His atonement for our sins and our receiving by faith His perfect righteousness, God wants us as holy before Him. Now God is at work in us by His Spirit, enabling us to grow more and more holy in our

lives. Because God counts us as holy, we "make every effort" by His Spirit "to be holy" (Hebrews 12:14).

8. Encourage participants to think of ways in which they are set apart for God in the way they live. Such things could include churchgoing, not taking part in immorality, keeping their language chaste and respectful toward the Lord, giving a portion of their income for evangelism and charity, wearing Christian jewelry, praying regularly, and many other practices and ways of life that require much or little from them. Be alert to support anyone who requests prayers or encouragement in an area of Christian living.

9. We're inundated in our world today by temptations that oppose holding on to God's grace: the prevalent attitude that there is no such thing as "sin"; that we're "all on different roads that lead to the same place"; works righteousness; indifference to feeding on the means of grace through regular church worship, and so on. As time permits, share other insights regarding temptations that make these admonitions in Hebrews appropriate also to our everyday lives.

10. (a) The writer was attempting to encourage his first readers not to back away from their faith and acknowledgment of Jesus as the Messiah in order to avoid persecution. He urges: Don't trade away the eternal blessings of your faith for temporary comfort and safety! (b) The writer urges us not to be foolish as Esau was and exchange God's love and grace for the pleasures and treasures of this life. He warns that there is no grace or forgiveness apart from Christ, and if we discard God's grace in Christ we have thrown away our only hope for life with God either in this life or in the one to come.

Day 4 • Hebrews 12:18–24

11. **Challenge question.** (a) Sinai is in the southern part of the Arabian peninsula; Mount Zion is in Jerusalem and symbolizes heaven. (b) Trumpet blast; loud, accusing voice of God; angel choirs singing glad praises. (c) Burning mountain, darkness, storm; angels and saints in joyful assembly around Jesus. (d) Terror and fear; joy. (e) Moses; Jesus. (f) Old priesthood and old message, condemnation, sin; Jesus' priesthood and message, forgiveness, grace. (g) Law, sin, condemnation; Gospel, grace, forgiveness.

12. Almost in an offhand manner the writer draws the most startling comparison of all. Blood, in the Old Testament, calls for punishment; specifically, the blood of Abel called for the punishment of Cain. "Whoever sheds the blood of man, by man shall his blood be shed" (Genesis 9:6).

13. Jesus' blood, the blood of the New Testament, the blood of the new covenant, calls for the forgiveness of sins. You might mention the words of the familiar hymn "Glory Be to Jesus" (*LW* 98:4): "Abel's blood for vengeance pleaded to the skies; but the blood of Jesus for our pardon cries."

14. *For personal reflection. Sharing optional.* Allow volunteers to share and discuss their responses, if they so wish.

Day 5 • Hebrews 12:25–29

15. As time permits, listen to two or more summaries. The purpose is to drive home the message of the verses: Mount Sinai quaked when God spoke to the Israelites in giving them the Ten Commandments and making His covenant with them. Not only the earth, but the heavens themselves shall shake and be destroyed when Jesus comes again in judgment, and only those who trust in Him will survive. If the people of Israel, who rejected God at Sinai, did not escape, how shall we escape if we reject Him who is our Savior and Judge?

16. After the Lord has wiped the universe clean with fire (a) God's Word will still remain (Matthew 24:35). (b) Believers' bodies and souls, united at the resurrection, will join Christ and the angels (1 Thessalonians 4:17). (Unbelievers will also survive, but they will join the devil and his evil angels in hell.) (c) A new heaven and a new earth, where righteousness will be at home, will replace the heaven and earth destroyed by fire (2 Peter 3:13).

17. Encourage participants to say what thrills them the most when they think of living in the age to come. Some may anticipate seeing Jesus, some meeting the saints, some reunion with loved ones, some enjoying the bliss of heaven, and so on.

Pilgrims' Worship

Hebrews 13

Preparing for the Session

Central Focus

Concluding his sermon-by-mail with various appeals, greetings, and blessings, the author gives concrete advice to pilgrims about their life of worship in thanksgiving to God.

Objectives

That participants, led by the Holy Spirit, will

1. understand and accept the exhortations addressed to them in this closing chapter of Hebrews;
2. desire to worship God with heart, lips, and life;
3. desire to be cooperative and obedient to spiritual leaders who speak the Word of God;
4. trust in the Lord Jesus Christ as the eternal and all-sufficient Savior.

For the Small-Group Leader

Bible Background

Even in this concluding chapter, where argument tends to yield more space to encouragement, the reliance on the Old Testament background is evident. One finds one quotation (Psalm 118:6–7 is quoted in Hebrews 13:6) and numerous allusions (to Deuteronomy 31:6 in 13:5; to Hosea 14:2 in 13:15; and to Ezekiel 37:26 in 13:20, to name a few).

But there is also one challenging passage that seems somewhat dark until one studies carefully the biblical background for it in the Old Testament. Hebrews 13:10–13 depends on several details in Leviticus 16. When the goat and bull were sacrificed on the Day of Atonement, the high priest brought the blood into the Most Holy Place. But, unlike the practice in the case of other sacrifices, the bodies of that bull and goat were taken outside the camp to be burned. Great sin and iniquity had been transferred onto them, and so their disgrace was borne outside the camp. The priests and worshipers did not eat the meat of these sacrifices. It is important to review Leviticus 16 once again for the study of Hebrews 13:10–13.

Small-Group Discussion Helps

The final chapter of the letter to the Hebrews winds up, as all Christian exhortations do, with instruction for daily life. The fact that there is a new and better message about a new and better covenant, the fact that we are the beneficiaries of all that Christ has made new, has applications for the way we live and move and have our being. The writer has appealed to us to "draw near" to this better way and to lay hold of it. He would have us now hang on to it as our way of life. These final words include, too, the benedictions with which Bible letters frequently conclude.

Day 1 • Hebrews 13:1–6

1. Some congregations have assisted in resettling refugees; this, perhaps, is a preeminent way in which congregations can practice hospitality. But there are many other ways, requiring less commitment but also important. Responding to local needs by providing housing, food, and other necessities is a way of practicing hospitality. So is providing temporary shelter for destitute travelers. Sometimes congregations are asked to provide lodging for visiting choirs, evangelism groups, conferences, or other church-related events.

2. In this exercise participants are invited to consider some Old Testament references to occasions when one of God's people received angels or the Lord Himself without being aware of it, at least not at first. In Genesis 18:1–19 Abraham played host to three guests, one of whom, though Abraham seems to have been unaware of it at first, was God Himself. In Judges 6:1–24 the host was Gideon, and his guest was the angel of the Lord (v. 20). In Judges 13:2–21 the wife of Manoah, and later her husband as well, received a man of God, who was, indeed, the angel of the Lord.

3. The separation of the people comes before any mention of kind deeds. That separation is made on the basis of God's grace in Christ, received by faith (John 3:18). But from genuine faith the kind deeds naturally flow, and Jesus here points to them as evidence of saving faith, evidence that all must acknowledge. Note that the "sheep" are surprised—for they had not done kind deeds in order to be saved, but because they already were saved; we're children of God by faith in Christ.

4. Paul compares the church to a human body. When one part of the body experiences pain, the rest of the body suffers as well. In the same way, Paul says, when one member of the church suffers, the other members of the church suffer too. That is also the point of Hebrews: "as if you yourselves were suffering" (13:3).

5. Perhaps nothing disrupts the well-being of a society as does infidelity within marriage. Families are broken up and children are deprived of a stable home, where they may be nurtured and provided security by both of their parents. More stable homes would benefit many areas of our society, from a reduced crime rate to greater productivity in the workplace. Participants will probably be able to come up with a long list of such benefits.

6. (a) Oftentimes envy caused by making comparisons with others disturbs our sense of contentment. When we see that others have more than we do, we may envy them and become discontent with what we have. Discontent may actually lead to dissatisfaction with God and a lack of faith in His love and care. Greed destroys our sense of contentment. Greed leads to materialism and covetousness. This is an old story that is still true. (b) The antidote for the discontent and greed that may lead even to falling away from God is faith in the promise He makes that He will never leave or forsake us. With confidence that the Lord is our helper, we will not be discontented or dissatisfied with the way God is treating us. If we have God, what more can we want or need?

Day 2 • Hebrews 13:7–8

7. (a–b) The writer to the Hebrews refers to the way of life and other ways in which Christian leaders evidenced their faith in a way that encouraged and inspired others. Allow participants to describe the faith-building example of those who have influenced them in this direction.

(c) Now help participants to put themselves in a different perspective and to think of those who look to them for spiritual leadership and guidance. These will include not only their children but new Christians and others.

8. There are many: the role of women in political and economic spheres; the way we think about time and space (five hours to travel from coast to coast!); the sanctity of life (with today's widespread acceptance of abortion and euthanasia); attitudes toward sexual behavior in public; racial tolerance. Give everyone a chance to share.

9. Here again, give everyone a chance. The realization of the extent and the speed with which our vocabulary has found it necessary to keep pace with the changes and the discoveries we have experienced is exciting and startling. Here are some possible answers: heart transplant; modem; fax machine; air conditioning; space satellite.

10. But Christ has not changed. He is still the same to believers today as He was to believers in the days of the apostles. Consider these statements: Christ came into the world to save sinners. He died for all. Jesus is the Son of God. Jesus will come again at the end of the age. Jesus was born of the Virgin Mary. Thank God, some things do not change!

11. We can know that, though the world around us should change, we can continue to depend on Jesus. He will continue to forgive us. In Him we will continue to find our strength and power. In Him we still find the grace of God. Thank God, some things do not change!

Day 3 • Hebrews 13:9–16

12. Participants might mention the New Age Movement or one of the various cults or charismatic groups within Christian churches or one of various new churches that center around a certain leader.

13. We are strengthened by grace when we continue to root our lives in Jesus and are built up by Him. This happens as the Holy Spirit sustains and nourishes our faith in Jesus through the preaching and teaching of the Gospel and through the use of the sacraments.

14. We receive the benefits of Christ's sacrifice through faith in Him, by believing in Him as our Savior.

15. (a) Christ suffered disgrace when He bore the sins of the world and was rejected by many of those He came to

save. Christians may also be called on to suffer rejection and humiliation in this world because of their faith in Christ. This evidently was the case with the first readers of this letter. The writer calls on them to suffer disgrace with Christ gladly, since He suffered disgrace for them. (b) Supportively listen to and, if so moved, be ready to pray for any group member currently suffering the disapproval of unbelievers, anyone mocked or made fun of, shunned, or otherwise suffering active persecution.

16. (a) The writer mentions two forms of sacrifice Christians may make as part of their worship. These are not sacrifices to make atonement for sin—atonement has already been made by Christ. These are sacrifices of thanksgiving and praise. One is the sacrifice of praise and worship, the kind of worship we give to God in services of worship. The other is the sacrifice of doing good to and sharing with other people for the sake of and in the name of Jesus. (b) Besides these sacrifices, the Bible also mentions a broken and contrite heart (Psalm 51:17); spiritual sacrifices (1 Peter 2:5); and our bodies as living sacrifices (Romans 12:1).

Day 4 • Hebrews 13:17–19

17. We are to obey spiritual leaders for the sake of the Word of God they speak to us. In obeying them when they speak and act on the basis of God's Word, we are actually obeying the Lord Himself, who speaks to us through the Word, of which these leaders are ministers, or servants.

18. When these leaders are able to fulfill their responsibility, everyone benefits. Our own spiritual welfare benefits, of course. The leaders also benefit, since they are able to fulfill their responsibility toward us more effectively, more easily, and more joyfully.

19. The writer seems to imply that he is being separated from his readers contrary to his will. Perhaps he has been imprisoned or is being detained in some way.

20. Encourage participants to put themselves in the shoes of one of their spiritual leaders. What would this spiritual leader desire? Quite possibly this will be that the participant will grow spiritually or be preserved in faith or exhibit a faithful Christian life. Such an exercise may help the participant see better the spiritual goals of the leader.

Day 5 • Hebrews 13:20–25

21. "Himself the victim and Himself the priest" we sing of Jesus in the communion hymn "Draw Near and Take the Body of the Lord" (*LW* 240). Our High Priest sacrificed Himself on the cross.

The Good Shepherd dies for the sheep and is also Himself the sacrificial Lamb "who takes away the sin of the world" (John 1:29). All these titles underscore His sacrificial death, "the blood of the eternal covenant" (Hebrews 13:20), by which Christ has redeemed us.

22. If the situation and mood of the group seems appropriate, pray for any needs that are shared. You, the leader, might speak the prayer. Or participants may spontaneously utter prayers for one another after the needs have surfaced. Or the group may pray silently.

23. Encourage participants to share an insight or understanding gained from their study of this letter.